Praise for
GREEN LIKE GOD

"Jonathan Merritt's GREEN LIKE GOD reintroduces us to a Savior who has eternal love for all of creation. Presenting biblical arguments, personal experiences, and hope for a restored earth, Merritt establishes himself as a prophetic voice for his generation and the entire church. This book aligns with a growing creation care movement that continues to turn heads and win hearts to Christ."

—Matthew Sleeth, MD, author of *Serve God, Save the Planet: A Christian Call to Action* and teacher in The Green Commission film series

"For too many years the concerns of the environment have fallen to the wayside among God's people. This timely book is a wake-up call to conservatives and liberals that caring for the planet is a responsibility we all share. May your own heart grow a size bigger and a shade greener as you read its pages."

—Margaret Feinberg, author of *Scouting the Divine: My Search for God in Wine, Wool, and Wild Honey*

"In my head, Jonathan Merritt will forever be a hybrid. With one foot on truths that are eons old and the other leaning into the future, he offers a combination of perspectives that is challenging, inspiring, and difficult to resist."

—Jonathan Acuff, blogger and author of *Stuff Christians Like*

"In this debut book, Jonathan Merritt brings together biblical integrity, Christian humility, and social sensitivity in a call to care for everything and everyone that God loves. Love God, cherish this world."

—David Neff, editor in chief, *Christianity Today*

"Jonathan Merritt has blown away political camps with good theology. He shows us the clear biblical evidence of a God who has a green thumb, a Creator who begins the human story by breathing life into dirt and ends the story with the restoration of all creation as New Jerusalem comes on earth. Here is a humble and clear call to all people to respond to the degradation of the earth, especially those of us who dare to call ourselves Christians."

—Shane Claiborne, activist and author

"Jonathan Merritt, already one of the leading voices on creation care in our nation, has written this wonderfully readable and personally engaging book. His explanation of biblical perspectives, his compelling personal story, and his practical action points all add up to a vital resource for any Christian sensing a moral responsibility to be a part of God's environmental solution. You've got to read this book!"

—Joel Hunter, pastor of Northland Church and author of *A New Kind of Conservative*

"GREEN LIKE GOD is a well-written, entertaining, and biblically faithful study of our great Creator and His marvelous creation. It will challenge and convict you. This is what a good book should do."

—Daniel Akin, president, Southeastern Baptist Theological Seminary, Wake Forest, NC

"Jonathan Merritt's book, GREEN LIKE GOD, is thoughtful, challenging, and engaging. And most importantly it is thoroughly Bible-based. It clearly lays out the sin of despoiling God's good creation and points Christians to a better, God-obeying way. If its message is taken to heart by American Christians, much will be done to save God's creation. And in the process Christians' witness to the world will be strengthened."

—Steve Monsma, research fellow, The Henry Institute for the Study of Christianity and Politics, Calvin College, and professor emeritus of political science, Pepperdine University

"Jonathan Merritt is a bold and persuasive spokesperson for our millennial generation. In GREEN LIKE GOD, he shows that creation care was a central part of God's plan from the very beginning and remains a priority for all of us today. Read this book and fall in love with the God who gives life and is making all things new."

—Ben Lowe, author of *Green Revolution* and cofounder of Renewal, a creation care network for college students

"By God's providential grace, Jonathan Merritt has become a voice of the under-thirty-five evangelical environmentalism. This wonderful book gives us glimpses into his personal journey into creation care as well as thoughtful theological and practical reflections on this critically important subject. I strongly recommend this richly biblical and devotional introduction to caring for God's creation. May it have a huge impact immediately on both the churches and the culture."

—David P. Gushee, distinguished professor of Christian ethics, Mercer University, and author of *The Future of Faith in American Politics: The Public Witness of the Evangelical Center*

"At a time when many faithful Jesus followers are rediscovering their calling to work for the common good comes Jonathan Merritt, who with humility and humor reminds us that loving people and loving God means caring for creation. A commitment to understand the plain meaning of the Bible and an ability to integrate Christian imperatives of evangelism, discipleship, scholarship, and compassion make Jonathan one of the most significant voices of a new generation."

—Rusty Pritchard, president of Flourish, a creation care organization for churches and families, and cofounder of the environmental studies program at Emory University

"Jonathan Merritt provides a helpful resource for Christians concerned about creation. Seeking to be both biblically faithful and culturally aware, GREEN LIKE GOD helps Christians navigate the often tumultuous and controversial waters. I recommend this book to pastors and leaders who desire to care more deeply about the creator and His creation."

—Ed Stetzer, author and president of LifeWay Research

GREEN LIKE GOD

UNLOCKING THE
DIVINE PLAN
FOR OUR PLANET

JONATHAN MERRITT

FaithWords

NEW YORK   BOSTON   NASHVILLE

Unless otherwise indicated, Scriptures are taken from the HOLY BIBLE: NEW INTERNATIONAL VERSION®. Copyright © 1973, 1978, 1984 by International Bible Society®. Used by permission of Zondervan Publishing House. All rights reserved.

Other versions quoted: The New American Standard Bible® (NASB), copyright © 1960, 1962, 1963, 1968, 1972, 1975, 1977, 1995 by The Lockman Foundation. Used by permission; The Holy Bible, English Standard Version (ESV), copyright © 2001 by Crossway Bibles, a division of Good News Publishers. Used by permission. All rights reserved; The Contemporary English Version® (CEV), copyright © 1995 American Bible Society. All rights reserved. The Holy Bible, New Living Translation (NLT), copyright © 1996, 2004. Used by permission of Tyndale House Publishers, Inc., Wheaton, Illinois 60189. All rights reserved; *The Message* (MSG). Copyright © 1993, 1994, 1995, 1996, 2000, 2001, 2002. Used by permission of NavPress Publishing Group; The Revised Standard Version (RSV). Copyright © 1949, 1952, 1971, 1973 by the Division of Christian Education of the National Council of the Churches of Christ in the U.S.A. Used by permission; The Holman Christian Standard Bible® (HCSB). Copyright © 2003, 2002, 2000, 1999 by Holman Bible Publishers. Used by permission. All rights reserved.

Printed on 20 percent recycled content paper using soy-based ink.

First Edition: April 2010

FaithWords
Hachette Book Group
237 Park Avenue
New York, NY 10017
www.faithwords.com

FaithWords is a division of Hachette Book Group, Inc.
The FaithWords name and logo are trademarks of Hachette Book Group, Inc.

Printed in the United States of America

10 9 8 7 6 5 4 3 2 1

Library of Congress Cataloging-in-Publication Data

Merritt, Jonathan.
    Green like God : unlocking the divine plan for our planet / Jonathan Merritt.
        p. cm
    ISBN 978-0-446-55725-2
    1. Nature—Religious aspects—Christianity.   2. Human ecology—Religious aspects—Christianity.   I. Title.
    BT695.5.M47 2010
    261.8′8—dc22
                                                                        2009041764

To Mom and Dad
For introducing me to Jesus and always believing in me....
even when it didn't make sense.

CONTENTS

ACKNOWLEDGMENTS

Books are often written in seclusion, but they are never the result of only one person's work. The ideas are often born out of community and then shaped by people God has placed in one's life. I want to express gratitude to all the people who helped nurture and shape this project. Many thanks to the following:

God. You are awesome. If I live a thousand lifetimes, I will never understand why You choose to bless me. I'm eternally thankful.

My family—Mom, Dad, James, Joshua—for encouraging me, supporting me, and pretending to be interested in every travel guide and book review I published along the way.

Erik Wolgemuth and everyone at Wolgemuth and Associates for working hard on this project to find it a good home and allowing me to drive you crazy with e-mails and phone calls during the process.

Joey Paul, Holly Halverson, Whitney Luken, Shanon Stowe, and the entire FaithWords team for taking a chance on a first-time author and being so great to work with.

Adrienne Ingrum, my editor, for bleeding all over my manuscript and taking the time to help me hone my craft.

Margaret Feinberg for being an amazing friend and mentor who selflessly taught me about what it means to be a writer of integrity, quality, and character. Thanks for challenging me to keep pushing when I was willing to settle for second best. There's a bit of your wisdom on every page.

Rusty Pritchard for teaching me everything I know about creation care and modeling the divine plan through the way you live your life.

Danny Akin for being a wise mentor who helped me discover my calling. You weren't afraid to tell me when I was wrong and lovingly guide me back to the right path. I'm so thankful.

Mark and Janet Sweeney for giving me a lifetime of knowledge about the publishing industry.

Everyone who listened to me read hours upon hours of my work and gave me thoughtful feedback: Lindsie Yancey, Katie Corbett, Jennifer McKay, Culvette Kunze, John and Ashley Welborn, Garet Robinson, Ryan Reid, Courtney Fahey, Ritchie Thurman, Sarah Manahan, Clayton Shaw, and Catherine Mileson.

All my teachers, mentors, editors, and encouragers who helped and inspired me over the years. Especially Larissa Arnault, John Hammett, Jim Jewell, Dean Inserra, Gabe Lyons, Mark Liederbach, Roxanne Wiemann, Corene Israel, David Gushee, Charles Detwiler, Leif Oines, Don Drollinger, Katie Paris, Joel Hunter, and Tyler Wigg-Stevenson.

For all the friends I left off this list and will remember in horror at 3 a.m.... I love you.

INTRODUCTION

God is green. The idea seems bizarre, almost trivial. Yet, I'm as sure of that statement as I am that two plus two is four and the mixing of red and yellow makes orange.

I didn't always believe it, though. It wasn't until I engaged in prayer, chance meetings with strangers, personal reflection, and discovery of oft-overlooked nuggets in Scripture that I discovered this amazing reality.

God loves and values His creation. God sustains the world and will redeem it according to His plan. Most astonishingly, God personally invites us into the process. For some time, Christian thinkers and leaders including Calvin DeWitt, Francis Schaeffer, Alister McGrath, and John Stott have called followers of Jesus to keep God at the center but Earth in plain sight. I stand on the shoulders of these giants and others as I write this book. Incredible organizations have also arisen to promote the biblical paradigm, which requires us to be protectors of God's creation and champions of justice. Yet work still needs to be done. Many Christians remain part of the problem even as God's Word empowers us to become a great portion of the solution.

As we work together to solve our world's many problems, we release redemptive power into the world. When we choose to live responsibly and sustainably, we bring hope to those whom our lifestyles affect. When faith enters the environmental conversation, simple issues become inspiring missions. When we become green like God, everything changes.

Environmentalists recognize the role faith must play in the conversation. Max Oelschlaeger, a professor at North Texas University, has written, "There are no solutions for the systemic causes of ecocrisis, at least in democratic societies, apart from religious narrative."[1] Edward O. Wilson, a famed scientist and Pulitzer Prize–winning environmentalist, penned *The Creation: An Appeal to Save Life on Earth*, a book that was written to a fictitious Southern Baptist pastor who Wilson believes might be the key to solving our problems.

But where do we begin? As an editorial in *Christianity Today* put it, "The Bible is not the enemy of the environmental cause, but its greatest asset."[2] Christianity has the most compelling religious narrative known to man, and that is why this book begins where it does—with a study of the Scriptures. In the pages that follow, we will encounter a divine plan for this planet, a plan I never knew existed. We will come face-to-face with mind-blowing problems all over the globe. Together we will survey the past as we search the Scriptures for God's heart. Then we will fast-forward to the future and consider those who will live on this earth long after you and I are dead, buried, and forgotten. When the church starts preaching and promoting the stewardship principles found in Scripture, humanity can really begin to solve our environmental problems.

God's people are on the move, and this book is your personal invitation to join in. The creation care movement views our world through God's eyes. It sees our environmental crises primarily as biblical and moral issues rather than economic, sociological, or political. The creation care movement seeks to honor God's heart for this planet and the people on it.

I've fallen in love with our green God. My prayer is that you will do the same while reading this book.

Enjoy.
JM

GREEN
LIKE
GOD

1

MY GREEN AWAKENING

I fell in love with our green God in an unlikely place: theology class. Seminary was an *unlikely* place because it's not typically where people fall in love—fall asleep, maybe, but not in love. Seminary has a tendency to be dull and heady, which has earned it the nickname "cemetery" among many. But my professors' passions energized me. History and theology were an invitation to me. I heard Martin Luther pounding nails into the Wittenberg Church door, I smelled the fragrance of atoning sacrifices burning on ancient altars, and I sat in horror with Mary at the foot of the cross. I developed an ever-deepening love for God during those years, but nowhere was this truer than in my theology classes.

Typical academic advice says that you should rotate professors each semester of theology to expose yourself to various perspectives, but I couldn't tear myself away from Dr. John Hammett. He was humble and fair. He was brilliant. Each class seemed to trim the hedge of my mind so that I left a bit raw and more refined. But one class trumped them all.

Dr. Hammett was talking about the ways God communicates with humans. "There are two forms of divine revelation: the special revelation in Scripture that is able to lead us to salvation and the general revelation we receive through nature. Both are from God," he declared over a scarred oak lectern. "So when we destroy creation, which is God's revelation, it's similar to tearing a page out of the Bible."

Wham! Wap! Bang! Like an action sequence from the old *Batman* show, I took one straight on the chin. Up until that moment, I hadn't been a friend of creation. I never recycled, and energy conservation was inconsequential. Although I never vocalized it, I believed that it was okay for others to struggle a little as long as I prospered. Prior to my classroom jolt, I remember tossing crumpled fast-food bags out of the windows of my speeding blue Pontiac thinking I was being bold and cute. When people in my car called me out for being destructive, I laughed. I often describe myself as a recovering anti-environmentalist.

As I sat in that theology class, God changed me. He began shifting my perspective and replacing it with His own. He stretched out His hand and grabbed hold of my heart. My mind returned to those destructive moments, and I felt God convict me of the sins of pride and selfishness.

Since then, God and I have had chats and encounters that have shaped me and moved my faith from belief to action. His surprising opinions about creation have leapt off my Bible's pages from Genesis to Revelation. His voice has nudged me to make personal lifestyle changes that I previously thought were reserved only for granola-eating, hairy-legged hippies. He has given me a passion for sharing His heart for creation—not as an "environmentalist" but as someone who is searching for

God's heart on these issues. He has opened doors for me to share with others in an attempt to build bridges.

I am just a regular "Joe" struggling to live out the whole Christian thing in an increasingly complex and broken world. I've never handcuffed myself to a tree, and you probably won't catch me wearing hemp anytime soon. You'd find some eco-hypocrisy in my life if you looked for it. I sometimes drive when I could easily walk, and I don't always choose the green option at the grocer. The trunk of my car teems with reusable canvas shopping bags, but I often forget them and am too lazy to go back.

I take a different approach. I won't attempt to make you feel guilty for having multiple children or eating meat or try to shock you with pictures of smokestacks and demolished rain forests. I won't bore you with "50 tips for greener living." This book is about the One behind the environment. It is as much about the Creator as the creation.

I am sharing my experience with this green God in the spirit that George Will penned *Restoration*—as a convert to a way of thinking with which I previously disagreed. I write as someone who has reflected on what Scripture says about all the things I see around me, attempting to listen attentively to the beat of God's heart. My journey in search of those divine palpitations began in seminary, but it became an ongoing mission to rediscover God's word and reevaluate God's world.

> I am sharing my experience with this green God in the spirit that George Will penned *Restoration*—as a convert to a way of thinking with which I previously disagreed.

When I look around me and see God's creation, the wonderment drives me to know Him more intimately. The way God has shaped mountains and provided ways to sustain life turns my attention to the artist who put it all together. Even His provision for mankind to eat from earth's bounty makes me hungry for Him. I want to crawl inside His mind and know what He was thinking when He fashioned it all. I want to ask Him what He thinks about all our environmental problems, and if He has a plan for how we should tackle them.

- Has God spoken about the nature of His creation?
- Does God have a plan for the environment?
- Is there a role He wants us to play?
- Is God really concerned about how we use His creation or if we abuse it?
- Did God make the earth solely as a resource to be consumed, or does it have inherent value worthy of preservation?
- Where does Jesus fit into all this stuff?

Finding the answers to these questions is indescribably valuable to me. When I purchase an important product that comes with a user's manual written by the inventor himself, I take some time to read it. The God who created everything has a plan for this planet, and I want to know what it is. I want to let the Creator's intentions and desires lead me on important environmental issues.

Many approach environmental concerns primarily from

a human perspective. Although their opinions are helpful, they aren't *supremely* important. We face unprecedented environmental crises today, and we need an "all hands on deck" approach to solving them. I want to see the stats and hear the experts, but as a follower of Christ what matters most to me is God's truth.

I left Dr. Hammett's class that day on a mission. I began combing the Scriptures for creation insights I never noticed. I read the Bible as if for the first time, and I wrote down every morsel regarding creation I had somehow missed before. Soon, the morsels made sense and a larger plan emerged. Though many of the truths I found seemed hidden or forgotten, they comprise a grand design for the world around us.

TOUR GUIDES AND TIRADES

As I wrestled with God's plan for this planet and the role He wanted me, and all humans, to fill, it naturally followed that I should survey the current condition of the world and apply my findings.

The true condition of our world shocked me. Millions die unnecessary deaths each year from lack of safe drinking water. The earth's diverse creatures, from tropical bugs to arctic animals, are facing extinction. Air in many of our most populated cities isn't fit to breathe. Dense rain forests, which hold medicinal power and incredible biodiversity, are being laid bare. Soil in many places is unfit for farming, landfills are piling up at incredible rates, and carbon emissions are at egregious levels.

A world of dire ecological problems is not a distant

reality. That is our world. Yet it is not until we view ecological problems through a divine lens that we can truly determine our obligations.

Christianity provides ample foundation for healthy living. But many Christians today are unequipped to live a life in tune with God's plan, unable to provide clear answers to questions people are asking about global problems. Other Christians shirk any responsibility that inhibits their free pursuit of pleasure.

> It is not until we view ecological problems through a divine lens that we can truly determine our obligations.

Unfortunately, many churches and pastors aren't responding. Some are doing nothing. Churches that claim to preach the whole Bible sheepishly avoid or brush over the many passages that reveal God's intentions for the earth. About half of all Protestant pastors in the United States say they speak to their church about creation care "rarely" or "never." That percentage rises to 77 percent for evangelical church pastors only.[1] I often wonder how so many pastors who are so rich in theology can be so poor in applying a theology of nature.

The poor application of this theology has had a trickle-down effect, producing Christian laity ambivalent about caring for God's handiwork. As one of the most sweeping studies of public attitudes toward environmentalism ever conducted states, "Evangelical self-identification is strongly associated with less support for the environment."[2] One modern historian adds, "Indifference toward the environment, or at least toward claims of environmental crisis, abounds in fundamentalist Protestant writings."[3] When one's commitment to conservative Christianity increases, coolness toward the environment often increases. A recent poll shows that Christians are one of the least likely groups to recycle.[4]

The church's unwillingness to address these issues also has had a trickle-up effect on those whom we elect. Legislators backed by the religious right consistently oppose environmental protections. In 2003, 45 U.S. senators and 186 congressmen earned an 80 to 100 percent approval rating from the nation's top Christian advocacy groups. But most of those same legislators received an average of less than 10 percent from the League of Conservation Voters.[5]

The discrepancy between Christians' attitudes toward environmental problems and God's plan inspired and motivated me. I felt compelled to do something, to play the part I felt God chose for me.

Great writers became tour guides, leading me along the path to environmental reality. I was astounded at the vastness of human-caused problems throughout the world, but more importantly, I was shocked at how blinded I had been to them until now. Living in a wealthy, first-world nation has sheltered me from the global problems that devastate billions of citizens of our planet. Living well above the poverty line has secluded me from many of the same problems afflicting less-privileged Americans. After my classroom epiphany, I felt impelled to act.

I contacted several Christian leaders and asked them to help me draft a theologically centered response to environmental problems. Once the document was drafted, I sent it around to leaders in my home denomination, the Southern Baptist Convention, asking for their support. The response was overwhelming, and in a few months, I released the final draft with the signatures of forty-six national leaders attached. I was proud of the input so many had offered that shaped the document, and I was inspired by the courage of so many to step out. I had no idea I had kicked the political hornets' nest.

Within hours of the document's release, my e-mail inbox was full. Some positive responses were sent, but the vitriolic tirades screamed louder. I was labeled a liberal, socialist, and tree hugger, and I was called names I wouldn't dare put in print. Leaders of Christian organizations in Washington, DC, threatened to ruin my reputation if I went ahead with this. People who claim to represent faith communities resorted to secular political tactics. I responded to these individuals the only way I knew how: with truths I found in God's Word and information about our environmental problems.

These things were indescribably difficult to process at the time. Everybody wants to be liked, even by people who don't know them well, and no one enjoys being called names. But the experience made me realize that we've built walls that must come down. We must do the hard work this important subject requires. We must mine the many nuggets in Scripture that address this issue and then apply them directly to the environmental situations in which we find ourselves. At the intersection of faith and facts, we sit at the feet of a green God who places the burden of action squarely upon our shoulders.

THE HIDDEN TRUTHS
IN GOD'S WORD

2

A DEEPER SHADE OF GREEN

I had spoken in front of large audiences before, but this was different. This was an assembly of college students, and having recently been a college student myself, I knew that it would be a tougher crowd than *Mystery Science Theater*. College students are easily bored and overly critical, eager to laugh and happy to do it at your expense if you give them the slightest reason.

A horn bellowed a high note and the band started playing, which signaled the procession. I marched behind the college president, who was robed in his academic regalia, as we entered an arena filled with more than a thousand students and faculty members.

I wondered why they invited me to be the keynote speaker for the school's annual convocation. The college's vice-president of admissions later said he selected me because he felt "a young face might connect better with the students" and because my passions and recent work corresponded to their chosen theme for the upcoming school year: "It's Easy Being Green." I felt they could have scored a well-known speaker with little effort.

Three months earlier, I had eagerly accepted the invitation, but my excitement soon turned to panic. I felt a lot of pressure to perform. The night I received the invitation, I couldn't stop pacing. "Looks like I have gotten myself into another mess again, Lord." I prayed that I wouldn't be boring and that God would find a way to use my message to impact someone. I even tried some breathing exercises I found on the Internet to help me relax. (In the end, I chugged some cold medicine and passed out.)

I spent countless hours during the weeks leading up to the event asking friends and colleagues for pointers on the best angle to attack the subject. I knew preparation was the key, so I began reading every book I could get my hands on in hopes that I would be ready for any postspeech questions. I collected heaps of material from others who had spoken in similar venues and on similar subjects. Finally, I scheduled a lunch with the vice-president to chat about the event.

We met at a local seafood joint not far from their campus. The VP said they were excited to have me speak as he slowly poked at his crab cake. I was curious to know what they were doing to promote the event.

He told me that each year his staff picked a theme for the school year, which they promote campus-wide. This year they chose environmentalism. To help the students begin the journey down the green path, they provided every student a copy of an environmental book and a green T-shirt with "It's easy being green" printed across the back. Every student would read the book and then listen to me unpack the whole "green thing" for him or her. It sounded like a solid plan, and I was happy to play a part. I looked forward to seeing the book.

When the book arrived, I had no idea what to expect. The school is a prestigious academic institution, so I assumed the book would be scholarly. I hoped it wouldn't be too thick. It is a Christian college, and I thought the book would perhaps take a juicy, theological angle, which I would love.

When the book arrived, I ripped open the package like a seven-year-old opening a gift from Santa. I pulled out a tiny book with a green, embossed cover.

I was stunned. With less than 150 pages of text between the covers, the slim volume seemed better suited for a coffee table than a classroom. I was also surprised by the book's content. It had nothing to do with theology. Each chapter concluded with an essay from a celebrity—Justin Timberlake, Cameron Diaz, Will Ferrell, Jennifer Aniston, and Ellen DeGeneres—on how to live green.

Slouching back in my red recliner and staring at the book, I asked myself: "What message is this book sending?" The only answer I came up with frustrated me: "You should 'go green' because it's cool."

THE GREEN TRAIN: ALL ABOARD

Where is America today? America is standing in a checkout lane with a pack of cool-looking, compact fluorescent lightbulbs. America is swinging by the neighborhood grocery store to snatch up a couple rolls of unbleached, recycled paper towels. America is not cold because she is wrapped in organic cotton and faux fur. America is not stranded on the side of the road because she is purchasing hybrid vehicles in record numbers. America is not hungry because she has been munching on gourmet organic snacks. America is bragging about these things everywhere from the homeowners' association to church events.

"Clearly, eco-awareness is no longer beardy, worthy, or dull," writes Mimi Spencer of the *Guardian*. "In one of the greatest retail revolutions of our times, it's hot. Green is glam. Sustainability is sexy."[1] Green is like the star high school quarterback of cultural movements. What was once reserved for Birkenstock-wearing flower children has hit mainstream culture. Green is the new black. It's trendy, en vogue, and cosmopolitan.

Like most trends, going green has become a source of pride. That's why, when you hear some people talk about how they have gone green, it sounds more like bragging than advocacy. I think about a lady I encountered not long ago at the mall. She was talking on her cell phone at a volume that invited, if not begged, me to eavesdrop. "Nonorganic milk?" she exclaimed with a mixture of Valley Girl drawl and utter disgust. "Eww! I wouldn't touch that stuff." She told her friend on the other end (and everyone within a hundred feet), in no uncertain terms, how much good she was doing for "the world."

According to the Institute for Grocery Distribution, nearly 70 percent of today's shoppers reach for more expensive grocery items if they are marked as organic, fair trade, or free range.[2] Sales of groceries labeled organic have grown by an unbelievable 20 percent a year for over a decade now.[3]

> Like most trends, going green has become a source of pride.

People are even eating green, and many are willing to pay big bucks to do so.

Everything from your neighborhood supermarket to couture fashion has been marked by the fad. An outdoor-wear company, Patagonia, produces fleece jackets made from recycled plastic bottles. Diane von Furstenberg, Oscar de la Renta, Nike, and Levi's all offer eco-friendly items. Even Sam's Club now sells organic jeans and T-shirts, making Wal-Mart the largest purchaser of organic cotton in the world as of 2006.[4]

The green revolution has even infiltrated corporate America where large companies fall all over themselves to at least appear to be environmentally conscious. Despite a struggling economy, executives strive to consume less energy, cut down on harmful emissions, and invest in sustainability. The computer juggernaut Dell is working with the Environmental Protection Agency (EPA) to lower its carbon emissions footprint and launched an ambitious reforestation program called "Plant a Forest for Me." Ten percent of the electricity at the company's Round Rock, Texas, headquarters already comes from renewable sources.[5]

Every time I turn on the television, it seems a celebrity is promoting his or her newest environmental pet project. Bono's wife has a line of environmentally responsible designer clothing named Edun ("nude" spelled backwards), Leonardo DiCaprio drives a relatively inexpensive hybrid, Julia Roberts wrapped her twins in eco-friendly diapers and lives in a solar-powered home, and Arnold Schwarzenegger has converted his Hummer to run on hydrogen fuel. Celebs have helped spread environmentalism well beyond the sandalista crowd by helping make it cool, if not sexy. "Have you joined the mainstream on this issue yet?" asks *Fortune* writer Adam Lashinsky in his article "Be Green—Everybody's Doing It."[6]

Even though Hollywood has thrown a red carpet over the green movement, if you step on it, you're likely to fall through. I picked up a recent issue of *Vanity Fair* that was devoted entirely to addressing environmental issues. The widely read periodical, which is loaded with ads for fashion lines, fragrances, and the latest Mercedes Benz, filled this special issue with tips and articles on going green. The magazine even went to the expense of hiring Annie Leibovitz to shoot a cover full of celebrities for the issue. Unfortunately, when it came down to taking its own advice, *Vanity Fair's* Lincoln Navigator–driving editor, Graydon Carter, decided to print the issue on less expensive, nonrecycled paper.[7] Carter knew a green issue would sell, but he didn't like the taste of this issue's medicine.

The message reverberating through culture beckons us to "go green" because we will look better and feel better and fit in, but the movement often feels flimsy and lacking moral foundation.

> 🍇 The message reverberating through culture beckons us to "go green" because we will look better and feel better and fit in.

TREND OR TRUTH?

I never want to run away from anything because it is considered cool or fun by the secular world. I also never want to run toward anything because it is considered glam-worthy. Some say the latter tendency is a mistake that many in my own generation have made, which produces faith communities indistinguishable from the rest of culture.

Both cultural separatism and cultural syncretism are unhealthy and unproductive.8 As a Christian, I want to enjoy many of mainstream culture's gifts and even participate in, contribute to, and shape culture. On my journey to a biblical understanding of creation care, I had to address the green fad. I immediately stumbled upon several problems.

Fads are fleeting. I've gone to the mall and purchased a stylish outfit or the latest electronic gadget, and by the time I got home, it was "so five minutes ago." Our world moves fast, and industries are always thinking ahead of us and making the "latest and greatest" quickly obsolete. Real problems that affect real people can't be latched onto a trend. Fads can't possibly outlive the problem.

Readers who are older than I may remember the hippie movement that peaked in the 1960s and 1970s. (For some of you, this time might be slightly hazy, but you may still remember parts of it!) Environmentalism was all the rage during these decades, much as it is today. The Clean Air Act was enacted and extended with support from both political parties; pictures of the earth taken by astronauts raised awareness of the earth as a sensitive, life-supporting ecosystem; and tens of thousands of American colleges and schools celebrated Earth Day for the first time.

Environmentalism then went to Washington and into the courts, leaving its grass roots behind. Professionals and lawyers were soon running the movement, and the regular folks were cut out of the process. As political tides changed, corporations became king and environmentalism lost its stylishness in the public consciousness. Popular support waned, and political parties began using the environment as a weapon to beat each other up. Clean air and water became greater problems, and land was clear-cut to make way for cookie-cutter neighborhoods. Today, eco-awareness is making a comeback. Unfortunately, problems of this magnitude don't come and go like fads do.

Fads fluctuate, but environmental problems require steady work and constant attention. If we take God's plan to care for creation seriously, we cannot do so because it is trendy. If that's our only motivation, we will find ourselves in dire straights tomorrow when public interest and attention have waned.

Another problem with pop environmentalism is that it's not accessible. I can't afford to fill my refrigerators and pantry with only organic groceries or buy one of those neat little hybrids. If going green means spending money—upgrade your vehicle, buy new energy-efficient appliances all at once, redo your wardrobe in organic cottons—some just can't afford it. Patagonia jackets and eco-friendly snacks are an option for those in the upper class, but to have a true impact on global issues, we must find globally accessible solutions.

Twentieth-century explorer and ecologist Jacques Yves Cousteau said, "The sea, the great unifier, is man's only hope. Now as never before, the old phrase has a literal meaning: We are all in the same boat." We *are* all in the same boat. We float together, and we sink together. The environment—whether polluted or healthy, preserved or exhausted—affects all humans, though not always at the same time or in the same ways. We are in this thing together, and we must work together to make a difference.

The biggest reason I reject pop environmentalism is because it cheapens the issue. We have deeper reasons to go green. We serve the Creator of the planet that green living preserves. He created this earth and took the time to tell us His plan for it. The God of this universe has given us the great task of caring for our planet. I like the way Charles Colson addresses this issue in his book *The Body*:

We should be contending for truth in every area of life. Not for power or because we are taken with some trendy cause, but humbly to bring glory to God. For this reason, Christians should be the most ardent ecologists. Not because we would rather save spotted owls than cut down trees whose bark provides lifesaving medicine, but because we are mandated to keep the Garden, to ensure that the beauty and grandeur God has reflected in nature is not despoiled...Francis of Assisi should be our role model, not Ted Turner or Ingrid Newkirk.[9]

> 🌿 We have deeper reasons to go green. We serve the Creator of the planet that green living preserves.

Why should we be consumed with a "trendy cause" when we have been given a sacred task? I encourage the things mentioned above. Energy-reducing lightbulbs, fuel-efficient vehicles, and organic foods are wonderful. The caution is not *what* we are doing, but *why* we are doing it.

Environmentalism takes many forms and draws from many motivations. At times, I find myself agreeing with someone of another religion or political persuasion about what should be done, but my motivation for doing it is vastly different. My motivation is God's truth. One of my best friends, Don, is an agnostic and tends to be rather liberal politically. I am an unashamed follower of Jesus Christ and tend to be more politically conservative. We often find ourselves agreeing more than we disagree, but although we agree about what to do, our motivations differ. (He says I am his "favorite Christian to hang out with." I am waiting for him to change his mind about that.)

When I think, act, respond, and live biblically, I have found people are disarmed—like my friend Don. When I am grounded in Scripture, my fellow Christians who view environmentalism as Earth worship, for example, begin to grasp the "theology of nature" and understand that I can't help but worship the Creator. They also realize that it is impossible to worship the Creator fully without valuing all of His creation.

A DEEPER GREEN

Until I met Dr. John Hammett and faced challenges like preparing for the college speech, I hadn't mapped out God's plan and didn't understand how much He loves this earth or why He loves it so much. I didn't understand the precious role we have been given to oversee the earth and help it to flourish. My speech that day went great, and even the cynical college students loved it—not because I am the best speaker, but because God has given me such illuminating material.

Psalm 119:105 says, "Your word is a lamp to my feet and

a light for my path." The Bible tells us how to live and why. It illuminates our steps and gives us a purpose for living. Our witness is most compelling when sacred Scripture drives it.

Our words will be most convincing if we offer deeper, more substantive solutions to our world's problems. While addressing environmental problems, ordained Baptist minister and journalist Bill Moyers wrote, "What we need to match the science of human health is what the ancient Israelites called 'hocma'—the science of the heart, the capacity to see, to feel."[10]

> Our words will be most convincing if we offer deeper, more substantive solutions to our world's problems.

Hocma is a Hebrew word that the Bible often translates as "wisdom." In the Scriptures, *hocma* is often found alongside justice, understanding, knowledge, discretion, prudence, humility, and faithfulness.[11] How different our world would be if our lives expressed those traits. How vividly our lives would contrast the uninspiring trends on magazine covers. Our approach to the planet would stun people if it were filled with wisdom, justice, knowledge, and humility. What would happen if we lived life in this deeper shade of green?

Moyers is right. We need to combine science and facts and figures and sometimes even trends with supernatural wisdom. But *hocma* ultimately comes from God. As the ancient King Solomon—someone who knew more about *hocma* than anyone who has ever lived—once remarked, "For the LORD gives wisdom; from His mouth come knowledge and understanding" (Prov. 2:6 NASB).

The world searches for truth in culture and history and science, but Christians know that the purest and most significant truths are found in Scripture. While the others are helpful, the Bible is our bedrock.

The trends and styles that culture exalts are not inherently wrong. That just isn't an optimal place to build a strong foundation for issues of this magnitude. We have an operator's manual for our planet right in front of us in the Bible, and we must allow that manual to change our thinking and behavior.

PLAN POINT: Rather than "going green" because it's trendy, God wants us to live according to the truth of His Word.

3

OUR GREEN CREATOR-GOD

I was unusually nervous as I entered the front doors of our church. Earlier that week, our associate pastor asked me to take over the morning announcements for our weekly worship services. The butterflies in my stomach were break-dancing. I don't know why a three-minute, scripted announcement made me so apprehensive. Perhaps it was just a bad cup of coffee, or maybe I have a hint of psychic clairvoyance and subconsciously knew what was going to happen next.

When I stepped through the doorway, I locked eyes with an elderly man whose stubbly face told me he'd skipped shaving that morning in order to arrive early. He was wearing a suit, and in our church, suits are not common. His salt-and-pepper hair was thinning. Though I was at least four inches taller, he was somehow able to look down at me as he spoke.

"You aren't gonna write any more articles on environmentalism, are you?" he asked.

"I…uh…well…I don't know what I will be writing on

in the coming months," I said, stunned by his brash question and that he would ask it in this most inappropriate place.

"Well," he barked, "we don't need any more Al Gores in this world. We already got one, so find something else to talk about."

What he said next is blurry in my memory because I was already planning my exit route. I only know that he was quoting facts and statistics and somehow ended up talking about some scientist at NASA. "So if you write anything else on that stuff, you'll be crucified and I'll be first in line to do it," he said. My head snapped back into the conversation. "Well, I guess that would put me in good company," I responded, looking him squarely in the eyes.

"Why the heck is everyone up in arms about the environment all of a sudden?" he asked. My posture was making my frustration apparent and perhaps contributed to the tinge of temperance in his voice. "When did all this tree-hugging start anyway?"

I paused.

"It all started in the beginning."

BEFORE THE LIGHTS CAME ON

In the beginning, nothing existed. Absolutely nothing. No air, no noise, no movement, no light, no material whatsoever. Silence hung like a Broadway theater in the hushed moment between the dimming of the houselights and the sound of the first words of the first scene.

Dark.

Formless.

Empty.

The anticipation was so thick you could cut it with a knife and serve it with a dollop of whipped cream. In a moment shrouded in mystery, God reached out of nothing and began to create. Land was born and the heavens appeared, "formless and empty" like a hunk of granite waiting to have a masterpiece released from within. Nothing became something, yet everything was still noticeably silent and dark.

God shattered the silence with words. At the sound of His voice, the curtain rose, and the stage was set for the drama of creation. The sole Actor emerged and began His monologue: "Let there be," He says. Over and over, God repeats this phrase or some variation (Gen. 1:3, 6, 9, 11, 14, 20, 24, 26).

- "Let there be light."
- "Let there be an expanse between the waters."
- "Let the water under the sky be gathered to one place, and let dry ground appear."
- "Let the land produce vegetation."
- "Let there be lights in the expanse of the sky to separate the day from the night."
- "Let the waters teem with living creatures."
- "Let the land produce living creatures according to their kinds."
- "Let us make man in our image."

God merely whispers a word and each time the Scriptures formulaically say "It was so." Existence follows words. This is the creative cycle. The Creator creates creation. God is creating something out of nothing!

The cycle is interrupted as God moves from creation to commentary: "God called the dry ground 'land' and the gathered waters He called 'seas.' And God saw that it was good" (Gen. 1:10). Rather than just creating and leaving us to figure out how valuable the world is, He stops to tell us how He sees the creation. He doesn't leave the significance of creation up to our imaginations or logic. God says plainly, "All this stuff that I took My time creating—that is good stuff."

God doesn't stop with land and water. In verse 18, God surveys the lights in the sky that divide day from night and comments that they are "good." In verse 20, God smiles on the birds and fish, which he also declares "good." In verse 25, God is so stirred by the wild animals and livestock that He takes time to call them "good." Accompanying each demonstration of God's power is a statement about God's passion for the planet, and after God constructs humankind He stops. In deep introspection, He looks back over everything He built and grins: "God saw all that he had made, and it was *very* good" (Gen. 1:31, emphasis added).

> Accompanying each demonstration of God's power is a statement about God's passion for the planet.

GOD, THE MAIN CHARACTER

The Bible is the awesome narrative of God throughout early history.[1] The main character of the Scriptures is our Creator-God, and He is always center stage. When I read the holy narrative I always first ask, "What does this tell me about *God?*" Only after I have uncovered the answer to that question can I begin applying the truths to myself.

The story of God throughout the Scriptures is about a creative, eternal Being who loves all of His creation, including us humans, and who is committed to the preservation and redemption of everything. We have been amazingly invited into this story filled with mystery, intrigue, and responsibility. If we do the hard work of stepping back and reading this story

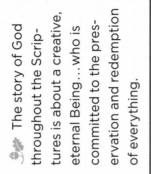

> The story of God throughout the Scriptures is about a creative, eternal Being...who is committed to the preservation and redemption of everything.

for what it is from its beginning, we uncover some incredible truths about God and, more specifically, about His plan for our planet.

One reason many do not know the divine plan for our planet is they do not understand the Bible. The Bible holds the answers to many of life's most important questions, but we shouldn't treat it as a fix-it book or self-help guide. Scripture is sufficient to guide humans in answering all of life's questions—including the most important question regarding eternity—but every answer to every technical question isn't found there.

Things get even more difficult when one dives into the Old Testament. Although the average preacher will spend most of his time behind a pulpit preaching exclusively from the New Testament, more than half of the Bible is comprised of the Old Testament—a literary compilation of war stories and divine intervention that reads something like *Beowulf.* How does one extract truth from this ancient storybook?[2]

One thing that has helped me is always remembering who

the main character is—God. Many people who read the Bible's story see the chronology but not the theology. They read the plot and never identify the main character. It is easy to read Scripture thinking the story is all about people. It is easy to ask, "What does this Bible story say about *us*?" But the Bible is not primarily about us; it is about Him. God is the hero of every story. When you first see Moses holding his staff over the sea as it parts, you think Moses is the hero, but then you realize that the first droplet doesn't even vibrate until God arrives on the scene.

GOD HAS POWER OVER OUR PLANET

I wondered why God started history's stopwatch with words. Why didn't He pull an *I Dream of Jeannie* and blink the universe into being? God could have created with a passing thought in a fraction of a millisecond, yet He chose to speak it into existence. He could have done it all in one day, yet He seems to stretch it out over six days. Why? If God could have created everything in a moment, why didn't He?

That God is able to create just by speaking exhibits His omnipotence. Yet He takes His time and speaks slowly. He stretches out the creation process as if to underscore the fragility and importance of what is occurring.

C. S. Lewis knew the importance of God's voice in this Genesis story, and he unveiled it when he retold the creation story allegorically in *The Magician's Nephew*:

In the darkness something was happening. A voice had begun to sing. It was very far away and Digory found it hard to decide from what direction it was coming.

Sometimes it seemed to come from all directions at once. Sometimes he almost thought it was coming out of the earth beneath them.... But, it was, beyond comparison, the most beautiful noise he had ever heard. It was so beautiful he could hardly bear it.

God speaks and mountains rumble out of prairie land, blades of grass punch through the topsoil and stretch toward heaven, and pomegranates swell on the limbs of a tree. With only a word from our God, horses gallop and snakes slither, winds whoosh and hot springs bubble. Like a skilled artist, God shapes the coastline and shades the sunset. Only God can command such authority over nature.

In the middle of a furious storm, the disciples cried out for Jesus, and with faintly more than a whisper, nature bowed down. It left the disciples slack-jawed: "Who is this? He commands even the winds and the water, and they obey him?" (Mark 4:41). But in reality, this question was answered from the very beginning. God reigns supreme over nature. Earth is His footstool (Isa. 66:1). Everything that occurs in the natural world is under His watch and control. "Not one [sparrow] will fall to the ground apart from the will of your Father" (Matt. 10:29).

By affirming God's place both before and above creation, we are also able to reject the popular new age and pantheistic streams of thought that claim nature is God and vice versa. God and nature are not blended together like a strawberry-banana smoothie so that one element is indistinct from the other. As the Anglican scholar N. T. Wright says, "God and the world are not the same thing, nor is everything simply held within something called 'god.' Within biblical theology it remains the case that the one living God created a world that is other than Himself, not contained within Himself."[3]

Even the name used for God in the first chapters of Genesis seems to emphasize His power. I am not one of those people who are real big on the names of God. But I *do* find significance in the name used for God in the creation story.[4]

Several names could have been used to describe God when He first appears on creation's stage, but the author chooses *Elohim*. This name for God is used more than twenty-five-hundred times in the Old Testament and is bursting with meaning. *Elohim* is actually a compound of two Hebrew words: *El*, meaning "strong one," and *Alah*, meaning "almighty." When the author of Genesis chooses the name *Elohim*, he is appropriately underscoring the Creator's unlimited power. As the prophet Jeremiah says, "Ah, Sovereign LORD, you have made the heavens and the earth by your great power and outstretched arm. Nothing is too hard for you" (Jer. 32:17).

When I was about seven years old, my parents took me to see David Copperfield's magic show at Atlanta's historic Fox Theatre. As a young boy who once asked his mom, "Do you think God would give me mutant superpowers like the X-men when I get to heaven if I ask?" I couldn't have been more excited.

"I heard Copperfield made the Statue of Liberty disappear," my dad would say with the same tone one tells a seven-year-old that the weatherman just spotted Santa's sleigh over Newark.

Once inside the theater, we followed an usher who pointed us to our seats with a waft of his flashlight. We waited for what seemed like an eternity until the lights dimmed and the music started. I'll never forget Copperfield coming out for the first time. He was liquid cool. Wearing a collarless black leather jacket and a white cashmere scarf, he cut bodies in half and wished them back together. With only the flick of a wrist, he teleported a motorcycle across the room. Sitting in my spring-loaded, red velvet seat with my jaw gaping in amazement, I thought, *Wow. David Copperfield must be the most powerful man in the world if he can perform such amazing feats.*

But Copperfield isn't powerful at all. He possesses no more potential to conjure magic than I did as a young boy. David Copperfield can't levitate anyone, and he can't make anything disappear. If you took away his mirrors and smoke and trapdoors, he might as well sell insurance. Like the rest of humanity, he cannot create anything. If you gave Copperfield nothing for building materials, the only thing he could construct would be a lengthy conversation.

On the other hand, our God can do anything and He created everything. He is an all-powerful Creator who, with the mere sound of His voice, can control the wind and waves and speak solar systems into existence.

God is unlike us. He does not chatter about or gossip mindlessly. When God speaks, it is beautiful and rich. It teems with knowledge. When God speaks, life is peeled back and truth ripples out. God's voice reverberates so that we can find our way—so that we can find His way.

In the opening pages of our sacred Scriptures, we meet a Creator who makes something out of nothing with only a few words.

The bedrock for the divine plan—the power and supremacy of God—is laid from Planet Earth's infant moments.

Those profound moments help us understand that our God is over and above everything we see. The bedrock for the divine plan—the power and supremacy of God—is laid from Planet Earth's infant moments.

GOD TAKES PLEASURE IN OUR PLANET

Five times in chapter 1 of Genesis, the author uses the word "create," a Hebrew verb ascribed exclusively to God, and in another five verses, the author uses the similar word "make." Yet in fourteen verses, we read that God "speaks." In other words, the characteristic action of God in this story is not creating, but speaking.[5] And when the Creator of the universe speaks, we should listen. For every time the Creator of the universe opens His mouth, we learn something of priceless value and importance.

I used to think that the Sierra Club was the first entity to recognize that the environment is valuable. But from the beginning, God tells us He approves of it. As noted earlier, God ascribes to it intrinsic value in Genesis 1:31: "God saw all that he had made, and it was very good." Notice that God didn't call it useful. When He first saw His creation, God deemed it good (Gen. 1:10) even though humans weren't around to make use of anything. God doesn't need us to make His creation good. God also doesn't say it is beautiful, although you don't need to see many purple horizons to realize that we are immersed in unspeakable beauty. Beyond its beauty and utility, creation maintains value and worth.

We know creation is good because we feel a stirring when we confront its beauty and depend on it for life. But even God, who depends on nothing, gives it a nod. If this simple passing comment on the value of creation were the only glimpse we had into God's heart, it would be enough to justify our fierce protection of the earth. But just to make sure we don't miss the point, God repeats it in verses 4, 10, 12, 18, 21, 25, and 31.

When God repeatedly comments that the creation is good, He is throwing up a brightly colored flag. When an ancient storyteller wanted to emphasize something, he or she would commonly use word repetition. The redundancy is like an exclamation point.[6] The writer is standing on his tiptoes, shouting. He is emphasizing these words to make sure that those of us who read the creation story millennia later don't miss the point that God takes pleasure in the goodness of His creation.

God's pleasure in His planet has powerful implications for us as well.

As John Calvin commented, "The repetition also denotes how wanton is the foolish contempt of man; otherwise it would have been enough to have said it once for all that God approved of his deeds. But God six times inculcates the same thing, that he may restrain, as with so many bridles, our restless audacity."[7]

To put this into perspective, think about a valuable human masterpiece like Leonardo da Vinci's momentous work *Mona Lisa.* Art historians and critics for hundreds of years have pondered and debated the complex simplicity of this work. Ever since his skilled hand reached for his canvas, da Vinci's homely woman has influenced the way others have created art. Can you imagine someone trying to make her quasi-smile more pronounced? Can you conceive of anyone painting highlights in her hair to make her look more modern? This would be unimaginable, if not appalling, in light of the excellence of da Vinci's work. Not only would the destruction or defacing of the *Mona Lisa* disrespect the artwork itself, it also would disrespect the artist who placed so much thought and work into its creation.

A masterful artist created the natural creation all around us, and it is stunningly beautiful, infinitely complex, and amazingly valuable. Even our survival is a testament to that. But the greatest Commentator and Creator of all time told us that it is a "very good" creation. Therefore, when we senselessly destroy God's valuable masterpiece, we disrespect the Creator who takes much pleasure in it.

When we fail to love creation through our lives, when we exploit it out of greed or apathy, we offend the God who made it. As the English poet, John Drinkwater wrote:

When you defile the pleasant streams
And the wild bird's abiding place,
You massacre a million dreams
And cast your spittle in God's face.

God treasures His creation so much that He intervenes to preserve it. The book of Job says the sun rises because God tells it to, God feeds the ravens when He hears their hungry cries, God watches over mountain goats and deer during their pregnancies until they give birth, and the eagles soar at His command (Job 39:12, 41, 27). God has even given every star a personal name (Ps. 147:4). Scripture says that God is

> A masterful artist created the natural creation all around us, and it is stunningly beautiful, infinitely complex, and amazingly valuable.

"loving toward all he has made" (Ps. 145:17). As Christians, we must love what God loves.

My older brother James and his wife, Natalie, recently had a son. When I held my nephew Harper in my arms moments after he was born, I couldn't imagine feeling any more love or pride for anything. He was fragile like a tower of fine china, and I held my breath as I handled him. In that moment, I didn't need anyone to tell me about the inherent goodness of God's creation. The pride and pleasure I felt gave this principle skin.

Yet as wonderful as Harper was at birth, God has placed in him amazing potential for improvement. He is talking and walking now. He knows my name. He's growing from a baby into a child, and one day he will be a man. He will learn to love, and he will develop his own unique sense of humor. If my brother and sister-in-law nurture and guide him correctly, Harper may become a devoted father, a dependable friend. He might one day be a steady-handed doctor, keen businessman, precise accountant, or, if he really does well, a writer. [8]

In order to extend the original goodness of this creation for the years that follow those first, sweet moments, his caretakers must do their part to nurture, care for, and protect him. Furthermore, when they entrust Harper to a schoolteacher or a babysitter, they rightfully expect them to use the same care. Harper's parents will make sure that the person in charge understands exactly what they expect when caring for their son.

Just as a schoolteacher or babysitter's proper treatment of your child would ultimately honor you as the parent, so our treatment of God's creation ultimately honors Him as the

Creator. God created an already good world and yet filled it with incredible potential. He buried within it provision and food and beauty and all kinds of bounty. God cares deeply for the well-being of His creation, and from the moment of its existence, He gives us a sneak peak of what is expected of us in helping it fulfill its potential.

"THE BEGINNING" IS *JUST* THE BEGINNING

The first chapter of the first book of the Bible sets Christians apart from other world religions and our own false thinking. Unlike pantheists and New Age environmentalists, Christians know God and nature are not equivalent. The Bible teaches us that God is different from and greater than His creation.

When I recognize God's power over our planet, I affirm His transcendence over the world. When I recognize that God takes pleasure in our planet, I affirm His immanence throughout the world. By keeping these in balance, we become stewards over creation rather than worshipers of nature.

The book of Job illustrates this principle poetically. On the one hand, the author of Job rejects the idea that God is equivalent to nature and calls Earth worship a sin:

> If I have regarded the sun in its radiance
> or the moon moving in splendor,
> so that my heart was secretly enticed
> and my hand offered them a kiss of homage,

> The Bible teaches us that God is different from and greater than His creation.

then these would be sins to be judged,

for I would have been unfaithful to God on high.

(Job 31:26–28)

I spoke recently at a "Religion and the Environment" forum at Meredith College in Raleigh, North Carolina. Joining me on the panel was an Episcopal priest, a Buddhist scholar, and a self-proclaimed theistic naturalist. I was representing conservative Christianity. The debate was lively.

My favorite part of the forum came in an exchange between the Buddhist scholar and myself. She was polite and airy, spoke in maxims and smiled perpetually, even when speaking. "I think Buddhism offers the greatest reasons to care for the earth," she said with a confident kindness. "After all, we believe in karma and reincarnation. If I don't do my part now then I might end up as a cockroach or something worse in my next life." The crowd nodded and hummed in agreement.

"I disagree," I responded. "I think Christianity offers the most compelling reasons to care for the earth, which all boils down to three words: 'In the beginning.'"

Unlike Buddhists, who believe that the world has no beginning and no end, Christians believe that a long time ago, the world began. We believe that nothing existed prior to creation, but with the sound of God's voice things came into being. As Christians, we believe in a God who is self-sufficient, so He didn't have to create the world; He wanted to. And we know from Scripture that God doesn't do anything without a purpose (Col. 1:15–20). He called this earth good, and He has a plan for keeping it that way.

Genesis has been called the "seed plot of the Bible" because it is the book that hatches many of our greatest doctrines from the Holy Trinity to justification by faith. The Bible's sixty-six books contain 1,189 chapters. The creation story begins in the first chapter of the first book. It is the front door to the rest of the Bible. As one theologian commented, "What we know about God, about creation, about ourselves, and about salvation begins in Genesis. It provides the theological pillars on which the rest of the Bible stands."[9]

The creation story was so familiar I could gloss over a reading without unearthing the important environmental message that comprises Genesis. When I engaged these Scriptures in a fresh way, I saw everything differently. When I rediscovered God's words in the opening act of this story, I realized God was telling me a whole lot about Himself and His plan for our planet, starting with the built-in goodness of everything I see.

Interwoven through all of the poetry and drama of this amazing story, God is displaying His illustrious power and stressing the immense pleasure He takes in His creation. And it is upon these foundational principles that the rest of the divine plan is constructed. In the opening chapter of Scripture, the audience is being prepared for what becomes an amazing story, a grand narrative. It is a story that doesn't end with restful Sabbath, but one that's just beginning.

PLAN POINT: Because God has power over and takes pleasure in our planet, we must recognize the Creator by caring for the creation that He has called "good."

4

DOMINION AS
BENEVOLENT MONARCHY

WHEN I turned fifteen, I couldn't wait to get my first job. At fifteen, you aren't qualified for much more than the fry station at Wendy's, and I am not much for fast food. My dad was pastor of the local Baptist church, so that seemed like a good place to begin. The only opening was in maintenance, and the job promised a paycheck.

This decision turned out to be a big mistake. The saying goes, "If something isn't broken, don't fix it," but I would add that if something is broken, don't call me. I'd rather curl up with a good book than a circular saw any day. Heat is my kryptonite, so attempting manual labor in the hot, humid state of Georgia bordered on batty. Regardless, I took the job and soon spent my miserable workdays daydreaming of two-week notices.

I actually don't remember much about that job, but I'll never forget the day I quit. I had been sent out to dig post-holes in the blistering heat. Sweat was dripping from my brow like a melting candle and my cheeks were burning so badly it felt like it was raining needles. About three in the afternoon, I paused and released a defeated sigh, dropped my posthole digger, and walked back into my boss's office. "I'm sorry, but I've had enough," I said without hesitation. He looked back at me with a grin that indicated he had been expecting this moment would come. I gathered my things and left...relieved.

Ten years later as I began combing the Scriptures for teachings on stewardship, I discovered something surprising: God had given me and every other person a job long before my first foray into the working world. My God-given job is something that I have been built for and am equipped to do—unlike digging postholes. It is a sacred task that God has given every member of humanity since the first person was created, and it is the basis of His plan for our planet.

> My God-given job is something that I have been built for and am equipped to do.

ADAM AND EDEN

Now the LORD God had planted a garden in the east, in Eden; and there he put the man he had formed. And the LORD God made all kinds of trees grow out of the ground—trees that were pleasing to the eye and good for food. In the middle of the garden were the tree of life and the tree of the knowledge of good and evil.... The LORD God took the man and put him in the Garden of Eden to work it and take care of it. And the LORD God commanded the man, "You are free to eat from any tree in the garden; but you must not eat from the tree of knowledge of good and evil, for when you eat of it you will surely die." (Genesis 2:8–9, 15–17)

When I was a kid, I would daydream about what it would have been like to live in the Garden of Eden. This happened most often while I was sitting in a doctor's office waiting room, gripping the blue flaps of *The Bible Story*. I used to pretend that I was leisurely walking around, eating grapes, dodging boredom, and debating with the lions on what I should name the orangutans. (Of course, in my innocent imagination, humans wore fig leaves even before the whole forbidden fruit-eating fiasco.) In my Eden, there wasn't much purpose for existence other than self-gratification. But this isn't the picture of the first garden that we find in the Bible. In Eden, humans have an important job.

Genesis 2:15 tells us why God placed humans in a garden—so we would "work it and take care of it." Other translations render that phrase:

- "Cultivate it and keep it" (NASB).
- "Tend it and watch over it" (NLT).
- "Work it and keep it" (ESV).
- "Take care of it and to look after it" (CEV).
- "Work it and watch over it" (HCSB).
- "Till it and keep it" (RSV).
- "Work the ground and keep it in order" (MSG).

God takes the time to craft a robust garden, which alone tells of His love for nature, but then He says the reason for putting Adam in it was so he would keep things in order. In

Genesis, Adam is both a real person and a representative for all mankind, so the charge for Adam to care for the world is really a charge to us all. Nowhere in Scripture is it ever revoked. The passage is clear and is reiterated in the chapter that follows (Gen. 3:23): humans are commanded by the Creator to care for His creation.

> The charge for Adam to care for the world is really a charge to us all. Nowhere in Scripture is it ever revoked.

DOMINION DEFINED

I didn't learn that truth when I first discovered the story of Adam and Eve and the garden as a child. I can't remember hearing many preachers in the evangelical tradition speak on that verse.

I do remember, however, hearing references to a different verse—Genesis 1:28—in which God says, "Be fruitful and increase in number; fill the earth and subdue it. Rule over the fish of the sea and the birds of the air and over every living creature that moves on the ground." Of the verses addressing our responsibility to the natural creation, this one often gets the most face time among some Christians because it has phrases that can be effective in turning back environmentalists.

"Subdue" and "rule over" sound a lot different from "tending" and "watching over."

Growing up I heard, "Well, the Bible says we are to have dominion over the earth." They were right, and that idea springs from this verse. The phrase "rule over" is rendered "have dominion over" in the King James Version. When this verse is overemphasized at the exclusion of the rest of Scripture, it can lead us to an imbalanced and human-centered ethic.

For an example of human-centered imbalance, I needed look no further than B. H. Carroll, the early twentieth-century Baptist pastor and cofounder of Southwestern Baptist Theological Seminary. In *An Interpretation of the English Bible*, an influential commentary popular among pastors in that day, he said:

In God's law neither man nor nation can hold title to neither land nor sea and let them remain undeveloped.... The ignorant savage cannot hold large territories of fertile land merely for a hunting ground. When the developer comes he must retire.... mere priority of occupancy on a given territory cannot be a barrier to the progress of civilization. Wealth has no right to buy a county, or state, or continent and turn it into a deer park. The earth is man's.

Carroll states, "The earth is man's" even though Psalm 24:1 clearly says, "The earth is the LORD's and everything in it, the world, and all who live in it."

It was difficult for me to believe that Carroll, a wonderful Bible scholar, would espouse this erroneous theology, common among Christians of his day, that nature is our enemy who must be conquered and enslaved.[1] This way of thinking is sadly still influential today and contributes to poor teaching and preaching on environmental subjects.

Some environmentalists on the other side have overemphasized Genesis 2:15 at the exclusion of Genesis 1:28. They speak only about tending, caring, and keeping but ignore ruling over and subduing. Just as theologians like Carroll probably never preached on Genesis 2:15, you'll rarely hear Christian environmentalists reference Genesis 1:28. What someone makes of our creation obligation often depends on which pair of action verbs they prefer. Do they favor our obligation to subdue and rule over creation or our obligation to care for and keep it? Answering this question will tell you an encyclopedia of information about the beliefs of a pastor, activist, theologian, environmentalist, or the loudmouth know-it-all sitting next to you in church.

When used selectively and in isolation, either of these passages can be effective in angry debate with biblical authority. This tactic makes for a good spectacle but is poor form. I am not a debater who only wants to win an argument, but a Christ-follower who desires to live by all the teachings of Scripture. I cannot pretend that either passage stands alone and cannot overemphasize the one that I find more palatable. A proper understanding of the divine plan must bring both passages into harmony.

The Bible is internally consistent, so a proper understanding of our responsibilities revealed in the creation narrative must harmonize Genesis 1:28 with 2:15. Remaining true to all the teachings of Scripture, I can't afford to approach these verses with the question "Which verse best fits with my beliefs?" and then elevate that one at the expense of the other. I must understand both as one harmonious command from a consistent God.

DOMINION NOT DOMINATION

In light of God's declaration that creation is good, it seemed strange to me that He would give us humans any responsibility for it. If He gave it value and He sustains it, won't He take care of it?

When we understand the Bible's teaching on dominion, we unlock an important truth about the divine plan for our planet. The Hebrew word for "subdue" literally means to take control of something. It is usually found in a political context in Scripture. Genesis 1 is the only place in the entire Old Testament where the object of this verb is the earth. The Hebrew word for "rule over" or "dominion" literally means to exercise a given authority over something. This word can be used to describe priests executing their duties or shepherds taking care of their sheep but is most often used to refer to the power of kings over their subjects.[2] We can infer, then, that Genesis 1:28 gives humans a monarch-like role over nature.

What was the role of a monarch in the Old Testament context? An Israelite king was unique. He was to be an uncommon ruler, different from the other nations. In 1 Samuel 8:6, the Israelites ask for a "king to judge us" like all the other nations. This apparently disappointed God and Samuel because Israel wasn't like all the other nations. Its ultimate ruler was God, and its earthly rulers weren't given carte blanche authority. An Israelite king wasn't to rule oppressively or be greedy. He was to remain a servant and subject of Almighty God (Deut. 17:16–20). When an Israelite king abused his dominion—when he got greedy, oppressed the people, or enslaved his subjects—God would judge and punish him.

As God gave dominion to Israelite kings, we have been given limited authority over the natural world. We don't have carte blanche power, but rather the privilege of responsibly enjoying the earth's many benefits and resources. This earthly domain is to be a place where God reigns above all. Every creature is to be treated with care. Humans are given the task of ruling the earth as "benevolent kings."[3]

In addition to the role God gives humans in Genesis, what He *doesn't* give us is important. Humans don't have sovereignty over the earth. God retains ultimate power of the planet, as discussed in the last chapter. The entire creation is still His even though we have been entrusted with a measure of authority. Environmental stewardship, as Scripture defines it, must take into account that at no point did God ever give humans ownership of the earth. He gave us authority. These are very different.

Unfortunately, a side effect of having authority is that it can cause one to be puffed up. It can cause us to strut around like the rooster in *Prayers from the Ark*, saying, "I am your servant, Lord, but don't forget, I make the sun rise." The rooster fails to recognize that the sun rises because God allows it to rise. The rooster becomes so confident in the job that God gave him that he forgets God altogether. I have to be careful not to become so confident in my God-given dominion that I begin acting as if God doesn't exist. The Creator maintains and retains sovereignty over the entire world that

> We don't have carte blanche power, but rather the privilege of responsibly enjoying the earth's many benefits and resources.

He first called "good." Without God, flowers don't bloom, trees don't bear fruit, and rain doesn't fall. God is sovereign.

Abraham Kuyper was a theologian and later became prime minister of the Netherlands. On October 20, 1880, he was asked to give the inaugural address for Amsterdam's Free University. Kuyper delivered one of his greatest utterances in the climax of his speech: "There is not a square inch in the whole domain of our human existence over which Christ, who is sovereign over *all*, does not cry: 'Mine!'"[4] Scripture's view of creation is consistent with Kuyper's view, not Carroll's.

Genesis 1:28 does not give us license to treat animals cruelly and use the earth however we wish as long as humans benefit from it. Abuse and neglect oppose the role God has given us. As one Jewish commentator puts it:

[Dominion] cannot include the license to exploit nature banefully, for the following reasons: the human race is not inherently sovereign, but enjoys its dominion solely by the grace of God. Furthermore, the model of kingship here presupposed is Israelite, according to which, the monarch does not possess unrestrained power and authority.[5]

Although God has given us a kingly role over the planet, remember what happened when God-appointed kings treated their subjects unfairly or pursued greedy ambitions.

Dominion as stewardship becomes clear in the second chapter of Genesis. We are told to "work" and "take care of" the earth. In a contemporary context, the idea of work has become utilitarian. We work to make a living and buy all the

stuff we need and want. We work to pay the bills and provide for those who depend on us. But the flavor of this command is different. Rather than working solely for ourselves,
the work described here preserves the creation.

Of the verbs in Genesis 2:15, Bible scholar Loren Wilkinson writes: "The significant thing about both words is that
they describe actions undertaken not primarily for the sake
of the doer, but for the sake of the object of the action. The
kind of tilling which is a *service* of the earth. The keeping
of the garden is not just for human comfort, but is a kind of
preservation."[6]

Wilkinson reminds us that we don't always have to connect environmental advocacy back to human benefit. Often,
preserving creation for creation's sake is enough. He rightly
connects stewardship with servanthood. Yet this statement is not complete. Although our execution of dominion
is of great benefit to the creation, it is ultimately done in
service to the Creator. 1 Corinthians 10:31 tells us to do
everything—even simple acts like eating and drinking—in
service to God. Godly ecology connects humanity's work
beyond the creation and back to the Creator. That's what
Genesis is conveying.

Understanding dominion as stewardship of God's handiwork rather than man-centered domination is consistent
with the original language. In the Hebrew, the words *work*
and *take care of* have much deeper significance, meaning to
work in ministry or to do something for God, to care for
diligently in obedience. Some biblical scholars even translate this verse to read "to worship and obey."[7]

We should care for this world, not primarily because it
benefits us and not even because it benefits an inherently

good creation, but out of obedience to the God who commands it. We care for His creation as worship for God the Creator. Another Hebrew word in this verse also supports this idea. When the author says that God "put" the man in the garden, he doesn't use the common term for "put" that we find in verse 8. He uses a term that literally means "to dedicate something in the presence of God."

For what purpose was humanity being dedicated? For service to God. Creation care directly benefits the earth and certainly serves the earth, but not ultimately. The work described here is worship, love, and obedience to the Creator. God has called us to be more than mere landscapers of creation; we are called to be worshipers of the Creator.

> God has called us to be more than mere landscapers of creation; we are called to be worshipers of the Creator.

MORE IMPORTANT THINGS TO DO

I have a good friend who runs through life as if it is a race that rewards the first one across the finish line with a dream vacation. For the purpose of this story, we'll call her Shelby. Shelby married early, and she already has several kids and a mortgage. She is living the so-called American dream, though she doesn't seem to enjoy it nearly as much as she thought she would. The idyllic world of picket fences, neighborhood parties, and Sunday pot roast quickly gave way to myriad bills, the shadow of mounting debt, and fast food in between soccer practice and ballet rehearsals. Shelby is a lot like most Americans.

Shelby doesn't recycle, her closet is chock full of name-brand clothes (with the price tags still affixed to many), her house runs on inefficient incandescent lightbulbs, and both she and her husband drive massive, gas-guzzling automobiles. She's a great mom and a fine wife, but she's a poor environmentalist.

Not long ago, I bumped into Shelby at a birthday party for a mutual friend. She looked frazzled, as if one of her kids just made her threaten to "turn this car around, mister." But she soon calmed down, and we talked about her complicated life. Financially, things were tight in her household. She felt crushed by a mountain of debt that had been accrued securing the "best life possible" for her kids. This led her to implement the fastest processes and cheapest products, which were often less sustainable. To cut costs in her household, she even stopped paying the local sanitation company to pick up her recycling and just threw everything in the regular garbage bin.

"I know that I should probably do more to 'go green,'" she guiltily said without my probing. "But I just have so many other important things that I need to take care of right now." As soon as she gets ahead of the curve financially and finds the time, she promised, her family will definitely be making some earth-friendly changes. Eighteen months later, she has yet to do anything to quicken the reality of these changes, I'm not holding my breath.

Most Americans don't hate the environment. They don't start forest fires just to watch them burn or refuse to carpool because they think the sky looks prettier with a sooty grey hue. They just think they have more important things to do.

They have to give their kids the "best life possible," which often means providing a suburban McMansion with all the trimmings and continuing to make the dreadfully long commute into the city where wages are greater so they can pay the bills. No one is completely immune from this way of thinking, including me.

Most of us want to care for the earth even though we don't actually attempt to live sustainably. Making changes that consider creation just isn't a priority to us right now. We live in a matrix of unsustainability that we didn't invent. It's hard to teach ourselves to live sustainably when everything in our consumeristic, materialistic society is tugging us in another direction. However, God tells us in the Bible's grand introduction that stewarding the earth is important. It is our human charge to farm, protect, and preserve it. It must be a priority to us because it is clearly a priority to God. Keeping important things important has always been a problem. Even the first human beings had serious priority issues.

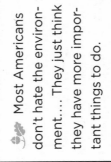 Most Americans don't hate the environment.… They just think they have more important things to do.

DOMINION ABUSE

The story goes that when God dropped Adam and Eve off in the garden, He simultaneously gave them both dominion and freedom. But freedom has limits. Luckily for the happy couple, God gave only one rule: don't eat from the tree of the knowledge of good and evil. But like a child who is told to stay out of the cookie jar, the first couple got caught placing their hands where they didn't belong: "When the woman saw that the fruit of the tree was good for food and pleasing to the eye, and also desirable for gaining wisdom, she took some and ate it. She also gave some to her husband, who was with her, and he ate it" (Gen. 3:6).

Several things happened at that moment. First and most importantly, sin infected the world, and humans suddenly needed redemption. But in addition to the fall of humanity, the earth also paid a price. As Christian ethicist Steve Monsma says, "Exactly in what ways the natural creation has suffered because of humankind's sin is open to question; the fact that it has suffered and is now corrupted and distorted is not."[8] The story goes on to say "The ground is cursed" because of Adam. We often overlook the fact that the first sin involved a tree, a vital part of creation. When Adam sinned, he didn't just sin against God, but also against creation.

I unearthed a hidden truth in this story: the first sin involved the misuse of dominion. At the heart of dominion is selfless service, but at the heart of sin, we find selfishness. Dominion is worshipful obedience while sin is irreverent disobedience. Dominion makes the Creator's will supreme while sin assumes that humankind's wills, wants, and wishes are paramount.

Original sin was essentially humans saying to God, "I know how to use Your creation better than You." For the

> 🍇 Dominion makes the Creator's will supreme while sin assumes that humankind's wills, wants, and wishes are paramount.

Christian, pollution should be defined as an act against creation that abuses our stewardship responsibility. When the sweet nectar of sin dribbled down Adam's chin, you might say, the first act of pollution was committed.

Evangelical scholar Francis Schaeffer pointed out the pollution-like qualities in this story. He understood the connection between original sin and dominion abuse. As Schaeffer says,

Since the Fall, man has exercised his dominion wrongly. He is a rebel who has set himself at the center of the universe. By creation, man has dominion, but as fallen creature, he has used that dominion wrongly. Because he is fallen, he exploits created things as though they were nothing in themselves, and as though he has an autonomous right to them.[9]

As a result of what happened that day, humankind maintains a sinful, fallen nature. We can't escape this reality for it is our state of being apart from Christ. As the poet George Herbert said, "I cried when I was born and every day shows why." At the same time, we remain called to be Earth's compassionate rulers, servants tasked with taking care of everything we see. Dominion is compassionate and caring stewardship and a part of what it means to live as God's servants. In awareness of these realities, we must be on alert so as not to exercise dominion as fallen beings apart from God.

Unlike my first job, the occupation God gives each of us is not something we can quit when we don't like what it requires. Dominion isn't our "Get Out of Stewardship Free" card. Dominion *is* stewardship. When we carry out this sacred task properly, we engage an ancient act of worship and place God where He deserves to be: above all else.

PLAN POINT: God has called us to be benevolent rulers, stewarding the earth compassionately in obedience and worship.

5

UNEXPECTED GOD-MOMENTS

AFTER graduating college with honors, I realized that honors didn't mean much to potential employers. A biology degree is about as useful as a degree in cat herding. Yet I somehow secured a job as a consultant with a large chemical company. I spent my days in a corporate mid-rise building with a good salary and the opportunity for advancement. Sound like a dream? Try a nightmare.

Meaningless work piled high on my desk, which sat in a cubicle on the fourth floor and, I'm thankful to say, faced a window. I was miserable. The only passion I felt between the hours of nine and five was when my clock finally signaled a lunch break. Day-to-day problems that were a bump in the road for the average person became mentally and emotionally taxing for me. Suddenly I felt eons older than every young person I met.

I had no idea what to do with my life, but I knew that what I was doing currently was not it. In some ways, I envied the family man who had a career and knew where life was leading him every morning when his feet hit the floor. My head swam. I felt like I stepped out of bed every morning and plunged into a spiraling free fall. It was as if I fell out of life's tree house called childhood only to crash through limbs of confusion and doubt on my way to the dusty, barren, and boring ground of adulthood. My uncertainty turned into panic.

"Why, God, did You put me in this situation?" He was supposed to be in control, but I couldn't feel Him in anything I did. Every morning seemed to bring a new frustration, a new failure.

Within six months of graduation, my roommate ended our lease, moved out of our Atlanta apartment, and returned to his home state of Delaware. Perhaps it was his disdain for city traffic, perhaps he just longed for poultry farms and wide open stretches of nothingness. Either way, I had no option but to move back in with my parents. As I dragged my feet into the house I had promised myself I would never move back to, I walked up the stairs to my childhood bedroom and plopped down on the bed in bewilderment. Reaching for my Bible, the pages fell open to the book of Ecclesiastes: "For everything there is a season, and a time for every matter under heaven" (Eccles. 3:1 ESV).

My eyes opened and I realized I'll never know the reason for everything, but I could always trust that God was allowing things to transpire for a reason. He gave me this season for a purpose. I was experiencing a bitter cold winter in my life, but as with the physical seasons, spring would eventually come. God was allowing misery as I pursued my plans, so I would begin searching for His plan.

Discontent is a fine motivator. Within months, I quit my

job, moved to North Carolina, began pursuing a writing career, and entered Southeastern Seminary where I enrolled in Dr. Hammett's seminary class and God opened my eyes to issues like this one. During this warmer season in my life, God gave me the wisdom of His Word and sparked a passion for things I'd never considered. A science geek became a writer; an "enemy of the environment" became an activist. God changed my life in ways I never predicted.

UNPREDICTABLE, BUT IN CONTROL

Of all the things I've grown to love most about God, topping the list is that He is so unexpected. Parting the Red Sea? Who would have predicted that one? Feeding a crowd from a child's lunch box? No way. Wrapping His only Son in human flesh? No one but God can take such eccentricity and squeeze out such profundity. Throughout Scripture, God shows up in strange and surprising ways. It is a mistake, however, to find only wonderment.

If I am not careful, I'll read these stories with fascination but never distill the transcendent elements. As clichéd as it sounds, everything God does is purposeful. In every surprising story is truth about God, His character, and His plans. But I must be willing to savor each passage long enough to discover what God wants to communicate. This is especially true in the narrative-rich Old Testament where we run into floating ax heads, talking donkeys, burning bushes, and dry fleeces on wet grass.

Regarding the divine plan for our planet, we have seen that God tells us a lot early on in Genesis. But He doesn't stop there. He continues to show up in unexpected ways to say surprising things about His heart for creation. Let's sift and savor a couple of these instances and digest the God-moments.

THE OLD MAN AND THE SEA

The story of Noah is without a doubt one of the most popular and most beloved stories in the Bible, but it is also one of the strangest. Noah's story is God telling a man who lives in a world where not even one one drop of rain has fallen to build a giant boat to house every kind of animal because He is going to flood the entire earth. If that isn't strange enough, God actually does it. He sends a crazy storm and floods the earth and wipes out everything that didn't board Noah's boat. Oh, and when it is all over, God puts on a psychedelic light show in the sky.

I've heard the story of Noah many times since I was a child, perhaps to my detriment because I take for granted how unexpected this God-encounter is. The great flood isn't just a story about "the man upstairs" blowing off some steam with a wicked rainstorm and some thunderbolts. It's a powerful tale of the Creator's mercy and grace and providence, a narrative about divine redemption and restoration wrapped with eccentricity so that we don't miss it. Noah's story is also rooted in history and covenant.

When I first learned the story in Genesis 6–9 at a young age, it went something like this:

Once upon a time in a faraway land, people's hearts were filled with wickedness. Everyone was so evil that God wished He never created them. God decided to destroy everything on Earth until one righteous man named Noah found favor in God's eyes. God was moved by Noah and decided to save the life on Earth.

God commissioned Noah to build a boat so his family and the earth's animals would survive a flood God was going to send. Noah did everything just as instructed and God kept His promise. Rain fell for forty days and nights until the whole earth was flooded. Every human except Noah and his family was killed.

Luckily, God remembered His promise and caused the waters to dry up so that humans could live again on dry land. God made a covenant with Noah promising never again to flood the whole earth. He placed a rainbow in the sky as a sign of His covenant. And everyone lived happily ever after.

The end.

If you learned a story similar to this one, you have a mostly accurate picture, incomplete in one seemingly small but profound way. In the childhood story, God made a covenant with Noah (that is to say humankind), but the actual story found in Genesis is different: "I Myself do establish My covenant with you, and with your descendants after you; *and with every living creature* that is with you" (Gen. 9:9–10 NASB, italics added).

God enters into a covenant with all the Earth. This is so important that God repeats it six times throughout the chapter! In verse 13, God says the rainbow is a "sign of a covenant between Me and the earth." In verse 15, God promises never to forget the covenant He has made "between Me and you and every living creature of all flesh" (NASB).

The covenant made here is not made with Noah. It is made with every living creature—indeed, the whole earth!

In this astonishing encounter with God, we learn a great deal about the divine plan. We see that God loves His creation and all the creatures contained within. Not only does He preserve them from destruction, but He also restores them and enters into covenant with them. God wants all of His creatures—not just humans—to survive and flourish on Planet Earth.

God's reminder to Noah to "be fruitful and increase in number" harkens back to the creation narrative and reinforces our role as benevolent monarchs (Gen. 1:28, 9:1). "To care for creation is in fact the first purposive statement that is made about the human species; it is our primary mission on the planet," says evangelical scholar Christopher Wright. "The covenant with Noah effectively renews this mission, within the context of God's own commitment to creation." Through God's covenant with the whole earth, we remember that God Himself acted to preserve the fruitfulness of nature.[1]

We also learn that God is the first and greatest recycler. He doesn't just throw away the good things He has made, but He purifies and restores them. In the story of Noah, we see "the foreshadowing of God's great story of redemption, the one that is still in progress within our own lives as followers of Jesus. And what comes through loud and clear is God's heart: He loves to recycle."[2] Thankfully, God isn't just interested in

> 🍇 The covenant made here is not made with Noah. It is made with every living creature—indeed, the whole earth!

recycling the earth itself; He takes supreme joy in restoring human souls through salvation found in Jesus Christ.

This Scripture reveals that God is committed to *all* life on earth.[3] God is definitely concerned about human beings, but He also loves the rest of creation dearly. He wants every living thing to be fruitful. Think about that next time you look up and see a rainbow.

 God is the first and greatest recycler.

DON'T SOIL IT FOR THE REST OF US

Throughout the Old Testament, God unexpectedly stops by to put the divine plan on display. In Leviticus 25, God gives Moses an unusual command:

Speak to the Israelites and say to them: "When you enter the land I am going to give you, the land itself must observe a Sabbath to the LORD. For six years sow your fields, and for six years prune your vineyards and gather their crops. But in the seventh year the land is to have a sabbath of rest, a sabbath to the LORD. Do not sow your fields or prune your vineyards." (Leviticus 25:1–4)

Eras before agriculturalists were writing books on crop rotation for healthy soil, God commanded His people to give the soil rest. The survival of His people would depend on their ability to manage the land properly. He protected all life by establishing a rhythm for farming. But also notice the repeated phrase in the passage above: "to the LORD."

Fruitfulness of the land was ultimately for God's benefit, not ours. Therefore, God prohibits land abuse.

Further support for this idea is found in Jeremiah 12:10–11 when he predicts the promised land will be abused by "shepherds" or foreign rulers. These rulers will make the land desolate. They will take something fruitful and turn it into something barren. The text says this is an offense, not only to Israel, but to God. Jeremiah even called people who have ravaged the land "vultures" or "destroyers."

God's command to steward the land properly was very serious. If the Israelites decided they would abuse the land to squeeze extra human benefits out of it, God threatened to punish them. He said He would curse the land with fruitlessness, send disease among the people, destroy their cattle, reject their worship offerings, and send foreign armies to exile them so the land could be forcibly rested (Lev. 26:14–35). God said, "I love the land I am giving you, so don't mistreat it. If you abuse My land, you will have to answer to Me."

Although the Old Testament law here may not still be operative today, God's character is. Hidden behind these teachings is God's love for His creation down to every speck of dirt.

What would happen if we had such a respect for land today? Would we still devour land by the square mile using armies of bulldozers without consulting God's plan? I am reminded of Isaiah 5:8: "Woe to you who add house to house and join field to field till no space is left and you live alone in the land."

> Hidden behind these teachings is God's love for His creation down to every speck of dirt.

Where I live in suburban Atlanta, you can't drive ten miles in any direction without passing by acre upon acre of land that has been cleared of all trees and had the topsoil removed, which sometimes takes thousands of years to replenish. Through our irrigation and cultivation practices, we often decimate the soil with restless work and harsh chemicals. What Paul Brooks said in *The Pursuit of Wilderness* in 1971 is still true: "In America today you can murder the land for private profit. You can leave the corpse for all to see, and nobody calls the cops." Developing land irresponsibly is not only ugly and shortsighted, it is offensive to God.

GOD THE GARDENER

I had the privilege recently of giving the invocation at the Garden Club of Georgia's annual convention. When I ascended the escalator to the banquet hall, a brigade of elderly women in unremitting conversation greeted me. Most of them wore bright colors, and many had fresh flowers hanging from their lapels. As I walked toward the main hall, I eavesdropped on random conversations about flowers and herbs and dirt quality. The churchlike warmness they shared with one another was special.[4] If God were physically living among us, I think He would probably be a member of the Garden Club.

God has always been a gardener. He planted the first flowers and cultivated the first garden, and He causes the earth's vegetation to bloom year after year. God chose to open and close the Bible in the same setting—a garden.

Perhaps the most peculiar appearance of God the Gardener is found in Deuteronomy 20:19 when God commands the Israelites, "When you lay siege to a city for a long time, fighting against it to capture it, do not destroy its trees by putting an ax to them, because you can eat their fruit. Do not cut them down. Are the trees of the field people, that you should besiege them?"

Here we learn the difference between using the land to survive and thrive, such as harvesting a field, and abusing land because it conveniently fits our purposes. We have the right to use the creation in order to meet our needs, but we never have the right to abuse the creation to satisfy our greeds.[5]

God tells the Israelite soldiers, "It's one thing for you to conquer your enemies, but leave My creation out of it. The trees haven't done anything to you." I wonder how our current wars would be different if we honored the principle here. How would modern warfare be different if we applied this mind-set to collateral environmental damage? It is easy for humans to see only human life as valuable, but God places value on His inanimate creations as well. Nonhuman life is valuable because God made it. Francis Schaeffer wrote, "The Christian stands in front of the tree and has the emotional reaction toward it, because the tree has a real value in itself being a creature made by God. I have this in common with the tree: we were made by God and not just cast up by chance."[6]

KEEPING AN EYE ON THE SPARROW

God is concerned about more than plants and dirt. He's also an avid animal lover. When the Israelites were enjoying an all-inclusive wilderness vacation, God oddly asks Moses to preserve the balance in animal populations, to be "a game warden of sorts."[7] Job and Deuteronomy reveal a respect and admiration for animals that we often overlook.

Psalm 50:10–11 (ESV) reminds us to whom the animals belong: "For every beast of the forest is mine, the cattle on a thousand hills. I know all the birds of the air, and all that moves in the field is mine."

God says, "I have created and care for the animals. They are good."

Proverbs 12:10 states our response to God's animal-loving heart in simple terms: "A righteous man cares for the needs of his animal." Solomon says that a person of character and righteousness—someone who reflects God's heart—is compassionate toward animals. In Genesis, we learn about caring for God's creation in a more functional way—as worship and obedience. Here, that function is being wrapped in emotion. We learn that living righteously means extending *kindness* toward creation.[8]

Proverbs says to respect animals, not romanticize them. Some today go well beyond respect. If they had it their way, eating meat would be punishable by death, and we'd all be feasting on tofu 'round the clock. As Christian thinker Karl Barth said, as we utilize animals for human purposes, we must do so with sympathy, such as a devoted horseman who is "so completely one with his horse that he always knows…what it can not only give but is willing and glad to give."[9]

John Wesley, founder of Methodism, noticed the injustice in mistreatment of animals. He asked, "Why should animals be subjected to suffering and violence when they committed no sin?"[10] Wesley believed that the way we treat our fellow creatures should reflect the value that God has given them.

All these fascinating words and surprising admonitions are woven together for this blanket statement: righteous people should extend God's love for animals in the forms of kindness, respect, and care. If the God of this universe takes time to consider the sparrow, shouldn't we? If He is looking out for every living thing, are we not required to do likewise as His image-bearers and ambassadors?

God's heart clearly beats for animals and plants and even the land itself. He implements rules to protect them and even intervenes to defend them. The idea that God places high value on every living thing knits much of the Scripture together. It was a crucial linchpin in Old Testament law, and it undergirds the divine plan by empowering us to promote habits, lifestyles, and legislation that respect all earthly life.

Christians often talk about the "sanctity of life." Let's take a step back and ask the foundational questions: Why is life so sacred? Is human life sacred because it is human? No. It is sacred because God created it, and He has placed value on it and it is the object of His love.[11] The Bible doesn't teach the sanctity of *human* life, but the sanctity of *all* life. Although plants and animals—from flowers to frogs—are not equivalents to humans, they remain creations of a God who loves them and has placed value on them.

Through Moses, God said, "I have set before you life and death, blessings and curses. Now choose life, so that

> The Bible doesn't teach the sanctity of *human* life, but the sanctity of *all* life.

you and your children may live and that you may love the LORD your God, listen to his voice, and hold fast to him" (Deut. 30:19–20). When we choose life, we choose to live in line with the divine plan. God demonstrates this repeatedly in Scripture, often in unexpected ways. If we refuse to let these moments stop at wonderment, we learn something immensely profound: God loves all living things.

PLAN POINT: God loves and values all life, and He desires that we protect and preserve it.

6

THE SANCTUARY
IN WHICH WE LIVE

BARBARA Brown Taylor says she doesn't
need to go to church to encounter God. A religion professor
and former parishioner, Taylor says she felt a stirring to rum-
mage for God outside of the church's four walls because she
and others were not satisfied with their weekly or biweekly
God-encounters.

We wanted more than set worship services or church
work could offer us.... We wanted more reliable ways
both to seek and stay in that presence—not for an hour
on Sunday morning or Wednesday afternoon but for
as much time as we could stand. And yet the only way
that most of us knew to get that was to spend more
time in church.

Taylor began looking for God in the natural world and
among everyday things. And she found that she could

develop a reverence for God just by sitting outside. During her journey, she experienced God's presence simply by taking walks along Hawaiian lava cliffs, sauntering in the North Georgia wilderness, and eating a fresh meal. These divine encounters reminded her that, in addition to the church on the corner, "The whole world is the house of God."

Taylor warns us of the limitations we place on God "when we build four walls—even four gorgeous walls—cap them with a steepled roof, and designate *that* the House of God." She asks, "What happens to the riverbanks, the mountaintops, the deserts, and the trees?"

In our suburban fortresses, we often forget that God is active in all of creation and that His character is revealed throughout the natural world. Perhaps the insulation experienced by twenty-first-century Western Christians keeps us from a more robust experience with the One we've given our lives to. "The people of God are not the only creatures capable of praising God, after all," Taylor says. "There are also wolves and seals. There are also wild geese and humpback whales. According to the Bible, even trees can clap their hands."[1]

Although Taylor and I differ theologically, her basic thesis hits the mark with the precision of a skilled archer. God has chosen to commune with us, and He doesn't choose to do so just in church. While His words flow from the lips of the ordained person standing behind a pulpit, they also resound from the many wonders of nature, which we rarely stop to admire.

> God has chosen to commune with us, and He doesn't choose to do so just in church.

Taylor's assertion that God makes Himself vibrantly known outside the four walls of a church is actually an ancient Christian teaching. Two thousand years ago, the apostle Paul wrote the following in the first chapter of Romans:

The wrath of God is being revealed from heaven against all the godlessness and wickedness of men who suppress the truth by their wickedness, since what may be known about God is plain to them, because God has made it plain to them. For since the creation of the world God's invisible qualities—His eternal power and divine nature—have been clearly seen, being understood from what has been made, so that men are without excuse. (Romans 1:18–20)

When Paul asserts that all of creation points us to God, he was building on a regular theme in the Hebrew Scriptures: God's revelation through the world around us. Paul, a well-educated Pharisee, would have meditated on Psalm 148:

Praise the LORD from the earth,
   you great sea creatures and all ocean depths,
lightning and hail, snow and clouds,
   stormy winds that do his bidding,
you mountains and all hills,
   fruit trees and all cedars,
wild animals and all cattle,

small creatures and flying birds.

…Let them praise the name of the LORD.

(Psalm 148:7–10, 13)

As a learned Jewish scholar, Paul would have doubtlessly recited the words of Psalm 19:

The heavens declare the glory of God;
　　the skies proclaim the work of his hands.
Day after day they pour forth speech;
　　night after night they display knowledge.
There is no speech or language
　　where their voice is not heard.

(Psalm 19:1–3)

I didn't need to go to seminary to learn about God's revelation. It was right there in front of me the whole time. As a child, I would eat fried pies made from the apples grown on trees in my grandparents' backyard. On family vacations, I would splash my dad and brothers in the Gulf of Mexico while fighting powerful ocean currents. In high school biology class, I pinned back the leathery skin of a formaldehyde-soaked frog to reveal astonishing complexity. At each juncture I was brushing up against God's attributes—order, creativity, complexity—even though I never appreciated it.

God speaks to us through His Word, and He also reveals volumes of information about Himself through the world we live in (2 Pet. 1:19–21; 2 Tim. 3:16–17; Heb. 1:1–3). We must attune our ears to creation's messages. The world is like a seashell; we must willingly place our ears up to its cusp if we want to hear the Divine rumbling.

A South Jersey farmer visited New York City not too long ago and took a tour of the Big Apple with a friend. They were standing in New York's theater district just off Broadway during the rush of the day. Car engines were roaring, people were shouting, feet were shuffling, and horns were honking. The wide-eyed farmer stopped and asked his buddy, "Do you hear that cricket?"

His companion wondered how the farmer possibly heard the song of such a minuscule insect.

The farmer remained still, likely squinting his eyes and straining his ears. He slowly took steps up an alleyway, motioning for his friend to follow. Finally, the farmer turned and looked down to see a tiny cricket hiding in the cracks of a brick building.

How did the farmer hear its faint music? The farmer's ears were sensitive to the cricket's melodies, having heard them many nights back on the farm. He was primed to listen to the sound. In the same way we must open all our senses to God around us.

The air we breathe, the water we drink, the food we eat: they miraculously bring us life day in and day out. We put seeds in the ground and somehow they grow into edible bounty—corn and wheat and rice. In the most simplistic yet fascinating cycle, water condenses in clouds and rain falls to the ground. It accumulates on mountaintops and flows down rivers into lakes. This happens each and every year with no prodding from us whatsoever. Without words, it is as if God is murmuring, "I am here and I will provide for you." The beauty of a sunset or the majesty of a snow-tipped mountain peak seems to echo, "I am here and I want to communicate with you."

Christians believe that God has written two books: world and Word. These books—nature and the Bible—are different in both form and function. Through creation, we know *about* God, but through the Bible, we can know God. We have access to God's glory through the world around us, but we have access to God's grace in salvation through the Bible. Both books are powerful and should be revered. The revelation of God through creation is so powerful and so obvious, Paul says that no one is excused for refusing to believe our Creator exists. The world is God's apologetic about Himself.

> The world is God's apologetic about Himself.

Bill Hybels, pastor of Willowcreek Community Church in Illinois, was on a sailboat with a cynical friend. Hybels had been talking to the man for years about the existence of God and the gospel of Jesus Christ. This particular day, they happened to be sailing across the water as the sun was setting. The colors of the sunset smeared a palette across the horizon.

"Now you look at this sunset. You look at the skyscape. And you look at the water that guys like you and me love to sail on," Hybels said. "Are you telling me that that's a cosmic accident? All of this?"

The man sat in silence for a minute pondering the question.

"Yeah, you're right," he replied.

"Well, let's talk about that God then, because He loves you," Hybels said.

Not long after that, Bill Hybels's friend committed to following Jesus. Floating in a boat and taking in a sunset, God reeled in this unbelieving fisherman. It wasn't logic that won him over. It was a simple moment looking out at a sunset that changed his entire perspective and that helped draw him into a previously unreachable God. [2]

Paddling to the middle of a lake at dusk isn't the only way to experience God. At 4:30 this morning, a furious lightning storm woke me from my sleep. Flashes of light penetrated my house and claps of thunder rattled my windows. I lay motionless for nearly an hour, hoping one of the tall, frail pine trees in my backyard wouldn't snap and send me running for the kitchen. The storm soon subsided and I reflected on God's mighty strength. The God who effortlessly controls the tempests' paths loves me. Humbled, I spent the next hour in Scripture, discovering more about Him. Even moments of fear in the midst of a storm, when properly perceived, can be a doorway to the transcendent. Through the tangible storm, I experienced our intangible God.

The great evangelical scholar John Stott said,

The God who in Himself is invisible and unknowable has made Himself both visible and knowable through what he has made. The creation is a visible disclosure of the invisible God, an intelligible disclosure of the otherwise unknown God. Just as artists reveal themselves in what they draw, paint and sculpt, so the Divine Artist has revealed Himself in His creation. [3]

SUNDOWN ON THE AFRICAN SAVANNA

My own sunset moment happened during a recent trip to Africa. Prior to landing in Dar Es Salaam, Tanzania, I had done what any BlackBerry addict would do: I activated international coverage on my cell phone. Though I had traveled with thirty-seven others halfway across the world to train pastors, distribute hygiene kits, and teach English, I was determined to stay connected to my life back home. My plan worked flawlessly until we spent the night on the African savanna.

As the bus bumped along through the gateway to the national park where we would be camping, I remember looking down and seeing my phone signal slip through my fingers as if I was squeezing Jell-O.

Four bars…no big deal.…

Three bars…surely it will recover.…

Two bars…does anyone have an antenna booster?

One bar…Please intervene, God.…

Blip.

Looking back on this experience, I realize that encountering a dead zone makes sense. The Tanzanian savanna is so flat, you could watch your dog run away for three weeks. At that moment, however, I was in a full-on panic. I stomped around the campsite with my BlackBerry in hand, trying to orient it toward the sky or at a satellite or at God, hoping upon hope that something would link up even for a moment. Finally, in frustrated surrender, I tossed the phone on my cot and went off, in a huff, to pout about it.

I walked to the edge of the campsite and sat on a rock facing the horizon. "Why won't my phone just work for a minute? I have e-mails I need to respond to and things I need to access," I griped to myself. "Why can't I make a connection?" Just as I finished my thought, I looked out at the horizon. The purplish sun was just setting, and in the distance, the silhouette of a giraffe was just barely visible. I was speechless.

I *was* making a connection. I was connecting with God. All around me, the attributes of God were tangible, and I was too distracted to absorb them. Like peeking into a view-finder, I thought back to moments in my life when God was all around me and I missed the opportunity to connect with Him in a fresh way. I thought about the culture we live in, all of modern life's distractions, and how we muffle God's voice every single day.

Surrounded by the world's toys and troubles, most of us walk through life unaware of nature's divine soundtrack. We are so busy treading the water of our schedules, we can't hear what God is saying in the natural world around us. This is why environmental issues matter to Christians. God infuses His own voice into the natural world because He wants us to listen to it and know Him better as a result. That God placed His revelation into the belly of creation indicates that His plan is for us to notice it and learn from it.

Think back to a time when you were in nature and felt extraordinarily close to God. You were caught off guard by something you might have otherwise passed by. Immersed in the good handiwork of the Almighty, your spiritual antenna was raised, and you caught a glimpse of the Creator.

All humans have access to the voice of God in nature. It is that stirring we feel when we stand at the ocean's edge at

> Surrounded by the world's toys and troubles, most of us walk through life unaware of nature's divine soundtrack.

midnight. We feel the lapping waves on our toes, which are half-buried amid millions of grains of sand, and we stare up at a moonbeam that stretches from outer space to our eyeballs. In moments like these we know we are part of something bigger, that Someone exists before whose splendor and power we are brought up short. We do well to experience these moments often.

Force yourself to take a moment and go where no one can find you. I have used the Blue Ridge Parkway when the leaves were changing for autumn, the front porch of a vacant house when the year's first snow was falling, and even a local park no more than ten square acres. The season doesn't matter and neither does the expanse as long as you are immersed in nature. Turn off your phone. Once you get there, turn off your MP3 player too. Be silent. Take Psalm 46:10 seriously: "Be still, and know that I am God." Ponder the things around you; ponder God. I guarantee the experience will do your heart and mind much good. It will make you more reverent, more grateful, and more aware of the One who stands behind the creation calling you to Himself.

If you are a parent, get your child outside. Don't let your children spend endless hours sucked into the mindless vortex of video games and television. A propensity to stay indoors has produced an epidemic becoming known as "Nature-Deficit Disorder," the inability of the youngest generation to connect with the natural world around them.[4] Although tragic on many levels, it is especially tragic because it means a whole generation may miss opportunities to connect with God who meets us in nature.

"A child who experiences the sense of wonder in the face of creation is learning, not only about nature, but about the glory of God," writes theologian Albert Mohler. "Children (and adults) who have no contact with the outdoor world are robbed of devotional knowledge, not just of natural interests."[5]

The natural world speaks to us in different ways than the Bible does because nature engages our senses. The Bible speaks often about the beauty of God (Ps. 27:4), but when I saw the sunset in Tanzania, God's beauty transcended words. You can read about God's power and provision and mercy and knowledge, but when you see these things reflected in the world (or people) around you, it becomes robust. Your understanding of God achieves a higher consciousness. Job once said he had only "heard" of God, but after pondering the natural order around him concluded that his eyes had "seen" God.[6]

A friend who is in the Army was recently sent to middle-of-nowhere, Arizona, for some training. Not having spent much time out West, I decided to visit and absorb all "The Grand Canyon State" has to offer. When I landed, the urge to buy a mass-produced Indian blanket overcame me. I bought two, which I stuffed into my luggage and tossed into the trunk of my friend's Hyundai.

We drove for several hours to the dusty, forgotten town where my friend was stationed and pulled into a small Spanish-style house. We unloaded the car, sat down on opposing chairs, and traded bewildered looks. The Grand Canyon was farther away than we originally gauged, and there were no attractions in this sparsely populated military town.

The sun had just fallen behind the horizon the first night when I began to feel stir crazy. The Microsoft Xbox had overheated, I finished reading all the magazines I purchased at the bookstore in the airport terminal, and there was nothing good on television. In a frustrated huff, I recovered one of my Indian blankets and dragged it out the door like Linus. If I wasn't going to see the Grand Canyon, I could at least enjoy the outdoors.

Lying atop my blanket, I wondered why I had flown across the country in the first place. There wasn't even Wi-Fi for my laptop.

Meditating on my misfortune, I looked up at the night sky and was besieged by beauty. I saw millions of stars, clusters and constellations that I didn't know existed. Atlanta's smog makes this experience nearly impossible. I was mesmerized, entranced by all the blue-white lights. I wanted to know their names.

The experience swept me with awe and humility. In a universe of such vastness, we are insignificant. Yet the God who created the vastness with a few words has chosen to love us. Suddenly Psalm 8:3–4 had special meaning:

When I consider your heavens,
    the work of your fingers,
the moon and the stars,
    which you have set in place,
what is man that you are mindful of him,
    the son of man that you care for him?

They say that some of the best stargazing in the United States is found in Arizona, but I say that great spiritual lessons can be found there. I realized that my flight had not been wasted. I had come to Arizona to experience God's beauty and power, to worship Him in a starlit sanctuary.

Had I not stopped to stare, I would have robbed myself of a profound encounter with God.

I'm usually so busy rushing through life trying to get ahead, I don't take the time to enjoy and absorb the things of God surrounding me. Such is the norm in America. We hustle to work and hustle home, pick up the kids from school and drop them off at soccer practice, race through the grocery store to make it home to watch *The Office* and never take time to experience God through the world. We don't stop to look at the stars anymore.

God wants to commune with us at all times, not just when we go to church. He has made the whole world His sanctuary. When we preserve nature, we can encounter God more easily. Natural revelation illuminates one of the *whys* behind the *what* of the divine plan. One of the reasons God is so protective of the earth and one of the reasons He charged us with keeping and caring for it is because He is singing through it, glorifying Himself in perpetuation. That alone should produce in us a deep appreciation for the creation and a passionate worship for the One who made it.

PLAN POINT: Because God powerfully reveals Himself through the creation around us, we should reflect on it and respond to it.

7

SKEPTICS, CYNICS, AND *NEW YORK TIMES* BESTSELLERS

I'LL never forget the craze over Dan Brown's book, *The Da Vinci Code*. Many Christians condemned Brown's work as irreverent propaganda. Perhaps the book's success contributed to this. During 2003 and 2004, it seemed every public space was painted with *Da Vinci Code* posters—from bookstore windows to Wal-Mart to church marquees. The book itself sold more than 60 million copies worldwide, and the subsequent movie, which landed an Oscar-winning director and lead actor, earned more than $217 million at the box office. (I'm still waiting for *The Purpose-Driven Life* movie to come out.)

Part of *The Code*'s buzz was due to its genre: faction, which is a hybrid mix of *fact* and *fiction*. The book was a novel (fiction)—the characters and plot were completely made up—but Dan Brown carefully weaved facts and theories about Christianity and Catholicism into the story line.

During the years when *The Da Vinci Code* dominated conversations, many people told me that Jesus was married to Mary Magdalene, with whom He had a child.

In Christendom today, faction ranges from harmless gossip to hazardous false doctrine. Someone says something that you know is false, but soon the whole church is repeating it as if it were gospel. You later find out that it wasn't true. Or you turn on your television to a televangelist's sermon and hear something painfully unorthodox. Take a pinch of Scripture, add a heap of faulty logic and—voilà—Christian faction that contaminates the church.

Misinformation swirls around these issues. Most of it is a halfway true piece of faction with the power to divert us from living as stewards. A good example of this is the misunderstanding of dominion, which we addressed in chapter 4. The arguments for man-centered dominion contain just enough truth to be dangerously convincing.

If you are like me, you have been on a steady diet of Christian faction for some time. Until recently, I held most of the positions I'm about to discuss. I ask that you keep an open mind as I offer what I believe is a better alternative to each, even if you have championed a few of them yourself. An ancient king once said, "The first to present his case seems right, till another comes forward and questions him" (Prov. 18:17).

> 🍇 Misinformation swirls around these issues. Most of it is a halfway true piece of faction with the power to divert us from living as stewards.

"ENVIRONMENTALISM IS FOR TREE-HUGGING SECULARIST LIBERALS"

Less than an hour before I began penning this chapter, I decided to run up to a local sandwich shop to grab some lunch. As I entered the door, I recognized an old friend of the family that I had not seen for quite some time. Our eyes locked, and she motioned for me to come over.

"I have been reading some of your writing, and I have to tell you how proud I am of you," she said.

I blushed and pretended I wanted her to stop flattering me.

"I just have one question: Are you *really* becoming a tree-hugging liberal?" she asked.

Environmentalist is a dirty word to some people. Like *Trekkie*, the word may be used in private but you don't want it on a personalized license plate. For some, environmentalism is synonymous with secularism, Gaia worship, New Ageism, and politically liberal special interest groups.

It is probably the most common argument I hear from people who have corresponded with me about this issue. Just as with the man who cornered me in the church foyer, I was fascinated to find that one of the most common phrases in the e-mails I receive is Al Gore. I have never said I support Al Gore. I have never made any public comments about the former vice president's work. Yet many assume that because I care about the health of our planet, I am "becoming an Al Gore."

Al Gore has a long-standing record on environmentalism that has made headlines for decades. As a U.S. congressman in 1978, Gore chaired some of the first hearings on toxic waste cleanup, and in 1990, he was a key supporter of the Clean Air Act. Two years later, Gore released one of the few mainstream pro-environment books at that time, *Earth in the Balance*. The following year, Gore worked with the Big Three automakers to launch the Partnership for a New Generation of Vehicles, an initiative with the goal of developing more fuel-efficient automobiles. While vice president from 1992 to 2000, Gore tackled such issues as safer drinking water, preservation of national reserves, and governmental tax credits for energy efficiency.[1] Most recently, he has been the most visible advocate for climate change. His work has twice landed him on the *New York Times* bestseller list and scored him an Oscar, Emmy, and Nobel Prize. These are not affirmations of Gore's work but simple facts about his involvement with environmental issues.

For a very long time, the liberal political bloc has been doing all the heavy environmental lifting. The organizations and individuals associated with this bloc often hold positions that devalue human life and accept a worldview that people are basically parasites on an otherwise healthy planet. Other environmentalists advocate for a radical animal rights agenda or support population control policies that Christians rightly reject. People whom conservative Christians oppose on other issues have traditionally championed environmentalism. We often mistrust environmentalism itself as a result.

Christ-followers find it increasingly difficult to ignore the environmental impact of their lifestyles and are beginning to feel a holy stirring as they wake up to crazy weather patterns, smoggy skylines, and disappearing forests, many Christians aren't comfortable with others who work on these issues and are even less comfortable with their proposed solutions. This predicament is one of my motivations for writing this book. The "radical left" has commandeered environmentalism partly because the "far right" gave up the moral high ground long ago in its exclusive pursuit of other issues.

My answer is to depolarize and depoliticize environmentalism. Caring for creation is not a right-left issue, but a moral-immoral issue that the people of God have been called to address. If we remain true to God's Word, Christians must with equanimity redeem the cause and make it our own. To leave these issues to secular environmentalists is to abandon our God-given responsibility to care for His planet.

God will not excuse our complacency because of our discomfort in partnering with individuals with whom we part ways on other issues. We must make progress where we agree and be "carefully eager about working with mainstream environmental groups."[2] We will be forced to develop biblical expressions of the mainstream environmental movement and offer alternative solutions to the problems we face.

Forcing environmentalism into a left-right dichotomy harms us all. If you consider yourself a conservative, you can remain a solid supporter of biblical values like the sanctity of life, but you should expand your political interests to include historically progressive issues like global poverty, human rights, and aggressive care for God's creation. If you consider

> Caring for creation is not a right-left issue, but a moral-immoral issue that the people of God have been called to address.

yourself more progressive, you can continue to support the political goals you find important while working with conservatives of mutual goodwill on issues like this one.

In a recent network news interview, I was asked which party I felt compelled to support as an outspoken Christian. I said, "That's the wrong question." The reporter was bewildered and asked for clarification. I responded, "As a Christian, I am not required to support a particular party. A better question is to ask, 'which *values* am I compelled to support?'"

Jesus never sided with the oppressive Roman government or the Jewish politicians who were even more divided than our American politicians. Maybe Jesus knew that great faith in political parties makes it easy to lose focus on the ultimate answer to our world's greatest problems. Let's not be divided over our party of choice. We don't have to be. Finding common ground on this issue rather than accepting a left-right polarity breeds hope for the realization of the divine plan.[3]

"THE WORLD IS GOING TO END ANYWAY"

For music lovers, the phrase "end of the world" conjures up riffs from REM's famous rock tune. For prophecy junkies and fans of the *Left Behind* series, it brings visions of the rapture and apocalyptic destruction of the earth by God. Some Christians use the "end times" as an excuse to shrug off earth care stewardship. Because Scripture teaches about an approaching apocalypse, the argument goes, then issues like depletion of natural resources and loss of biodiversity are inconsequential. "As much as environmentalists try to save the earth, their efforts will ultimately end in total failure. The Bible predicts that during the tribulation hour, the world will come to near complete ruin," says Todd Strandberg of RaptureReady .com. "I am strongly against Christians embracing the environmental movement."[4]

Anglican Bishop N. T. Wright ran into this line of thinking during a recent visit to Ontario, Canada:

Many conservative Christians in the area, and more importantly just to the South in the United States, had been urging that since we were living in the end times, with the world about to come to an end, there was no point worrying about trying to stop polluting the planet with acid rain and the like. Indeed, wasn't it unspiritual and even a sign of a lack of faith, to think about such things? If God was intending to bring the whole world to a shuddering halt, what was the problem? If Armageddon was just around the corner, it didn't matter—and here, I suspect, is part of the real agenda—if General Motors went on pumping poisonous gases into the Canadian atmosphere.[5]

Why worry about the future of an earth that has no future? Try applying it to another element of God's creation like the human body: *My body will ultimately be glorified so I'll treat it poorly in the meantime: I'll smoke a pack of cigarettes a day because I am going to die one day anyway.* Ridiculous! Future knowledge doesn't change our present obligations. Our stewardship responsibilities transcend our eschatology— our theology about end times. Many Christians believe that the earth will not be destroyed, but renewed and perfected. Neither scenario revokes our stewardship responsibility. I believe that one day Jesus will return to renew and restore the earth, but in the meantime, we are told to live in worship of and obedience to Him.

I struggled with this when I first started investigating creation care. Then I came across a story that I had read a hundred times, which I now applied in a fresh way. The tale is about a very wealthy man who was going away on a long business trip. Before he left, he called together his servants and divvied up his money to them:

To one he gave five talents of money, to another two talents, and to another one talent, each according to his ability. Then he went on his journey. The man who had received five talents went at once and put his money to work and gained five more. So also, the one with the two talents gained two more. But the man who had received the one talent went off, dug a hole in the ground and hid his master's money. After a long time the master of those servants returned and settled accounts with them. (Matthew 25:15–19)

When the businessman found out that the first two had taken good care of what he gave them, he was overjoyed and said, "Well done, good and faithful servant! You have been faithful with a few things; I will put you in charge of many things. Come and share your master's happiness." Then the businessman turned to the third servant, the one who dug a hole and buried his money in the ground. This servant hid his talent and didn't help it grow, develop, and flourish. And how did the master respond? He became very angry and called him a "wicked, lazy servant" (Matt. 25:23, 26).

This story is, of course, one of Jesus' most famous parables, and it teaches a very important lesson to those who claim that we can bury our obligations to this planet because Christ is going to return soon. The knowledge of a returning Master does not free us from our earthly obligations; it calls us to them.

One day, every person will be judged on all aspects

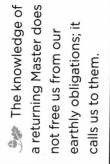

> The knowledge of a returning Master does not free us from our earthly obligations; it calls us to them.

of his life, and as the book of Revelation says, there will even be a time for "destroying those who destroy the earth" (Rev. 11:18). When Christ returns, He wants to find us faithfully doing all the things He asked us to do. He is going to be concerned with what we did with all His "stuff" while He was gone. Did we nurture it and help it thrive or did we simply forget about it and go about our lives? As Francis Schaeffer said, "A Christian-based science and technology should consciously try to see nature substantially healed, while waiting for the future complete healing at Christ's return."[6]

When those clouds peel back and my Savior returns to this planet, I want to be caught in the act of loving people, worshiping Christ, and obeying all God's commands, including the command to care for His creation.

"CREATION CARE DISTRACTS US FROM MORE IMPORTANT TASKS"

One of the most divisive environmental issues around is global climate change. (For more on this, check out

Appendix 2.) It has divided politicians for decades and has recently begun dividing the Christian community. Shortly before his death, the founder of the Moral Majority, Jerry Falwell, preached a sermon entitled "The Myth of Global Warming," at Thomas Road Baptist Church in which he addressed the issue head-on: "If I decide here as the pastor and our deacons decide that we're going to get caught up in the global warming thing, we're not going to be able to reach the masses of souls for Christ, because our attention will be elsewhere," he declared from the pulpit. "That's pretty wise for Satan to concoct."[7]

Christians are charged with the task of evangelizing the world, the argument goes, so we can't let environmental issues distract us from our true mission. They say that we have to choose between evangelism and creation care, and therefore, we must pick evangelism.

We aren't forced to choose between sharing the gospel and creation care. It is a false dichotomy. Both are possible. The very fact that the Bible tells us to do both indicates that evangelism and creation care can simultaneously be done well. A vital part of the Great Commission reaches beyond making converts to making disciples teaching them to observe all God commands, including the very first commands to steward the earth.

Creation care is a gospel issue. Shortly after several Southern Baptist leaders released a statement on creation care, I began receiving e-mails from International Mission Board missionaries telling me how relieved they were to see this. From Canada to Slovenia, from Brazil to Ukraine, I felt a virtual exhale. In many places on the mission field, our missionaries don't begin with Jesus, whom some foreigners know nothing about. They begin with the creation (and its Creator), which we know communicates with everyone.

Creation care speaks to people in developing nations where people have a greater connection to nature in everyday life. Creation care is a bridge for the gospel in these places. But it also bolsters the gospel in the Western world where many people know of, if not respect, Jesus. People aren't as connected with creation in these places, but they are often more familiar with Christianity. The whole world is increasingly equating an externally focused, sustainable, earth-friendly lifestyle with what it means to be a "good person." When the world sees the Christian community perpetuating systems of wealth and waste, it damages our witness. When they see us living compassionate, sustainable lives, our witness becomes authentic and convincing.

> When the world sees the Christian community perpetuating systems of wealth and waste, it damages our witness.

Rand Clark planted Genesis Church in Castle Rock, Colorado, in the belief that the gospel and creation care are inextricably connected. Rather than care only for people, the ethos of his church is to care for everything and everyone in their community. During their annual event, "Spring Up the Creek," they restore a local river that has become an illegal dumping ground. Genesis's sports ministry pries children away from the television and connects them with the outdoors. During "Trash Bash," congregants pick up garbage along a local highway they've adopted. "Cans for Clean Water" is a program in association with neighborhood associations to collect aluminum cans to be recycled.

The money received from the recycling center is donated to a clean water project in Sudan.

Not only is Genesis Church obeying the creation care teachings in Scripture, it has developed a unique platform on which to share the gospel. Rand tells me that people are always asking why they do such things, which begins a great conversation about salvation found in Jesus. Just as Paul found a natural connection point with the Greek culture in Acts 17, Rand believes we can do the same thing through living as stewards in the twenty-first century.

What we say and how we live speak volumes about who we really are as Christians and whom we represent. A Japanese proverb says, "The reputation of a thousand years may be determined by the conduct of one hour." And as Americans, we also have a great responsibility because of our association with Christianity. The way Americans behave is noted by others around the world, so when Americans are unruly, Christianity suffers. More is at stake than just spotted owls, snail darters, and a few degrees Fahrenheit. Our integrity, our witness, and our credibility are at risk.

My agnostic friend Don once remarked that one of the things that most discourages him from becoming a Christian is the hypocrisy of the Christian community in how it responds to social issues like environmentalism. "If you Christians truly believe that God exists and if you really believe that God made the world for everyone to live on, then why does it seem like you don't care about preserving it?" Don once asked me. "Wouldn't that be like destroying the playhouse your dad built for you?" I believe his analogy expresses the sentiments felt by many religious skeptics. As Christians and as Americans, our responsibility is clearly great. We aren't forced to choose between proclaiming the Word of God and carrying out the work God has given us to do. When done properly and proportionately, creation care serves only to strengthen the gospel.

WAS JESUS GREEN?

As 2009 was dawning and President Obama was about to take the reins of our country, political pundits from both sides were working overtime. Every time I turned on the television or radio, they would be reflecting on the past administration, arguing about our present realities, and predicting what the future would be like under the new commander-in-chief. Among the hot-button issues that were panicking the pundits, the war in Iraq seemed to top the list. After all, the war was dragging on at a pace even Aesop would question, and Americans were beginning to get antsy. A lightbulb came on over the head of my inner journalist. (It was a compact fluorescent lightbulb, of course.)

I decided to write an article for *Relevant* magazine on how Christians should view war. Because I am not an expert on the issue, I called a good friend who teaches ethics at a well-known university. He has written books on the subject, so I figured he would be a natural starting point. My friend was helping me write the interview questions, and as he spoke, I wrote furiously. As we were about to get off the phone, he said something so simple yet so profound it embarrassed me for not having already thought about it.

"All the questions I have given you are very important," he said. "But the most important question you can ask is, 'Where is Jesus in your theory?'"

I've never asked that question of anyone. I have written more than a hundred articles on dozens of issues for publications in both the Christian and secular world, but I had never asked where Jesus came into the picture. In one sense, it occurred to me, every article I published until that day had fallen short.

People who are skeptical of all things green love to point out that Jesus never directly addressed environmentalism, and in one sense, they are correct. Jesus never reiterated the Genesis 2:15 charge to keep and care for the earth. He never overturned the tables of greedy developers, and not once did He rebuke a Jewish farmer for unsustainable practices. Jesus never preached a single sermon on environmental stewardship. Trust me, I've looked for it.

Jesus is the supreme revelation of God, He is the foundation of our faith, He is the reason for our hope, He is the greatest teacher who ever lived, and He is the basis for everything we believe. The teachings of Jesus Christ must be at the heart of any Christian paradigm. More directly, if we believe that God has a plan for our planet and we have a role to play, Jesus must be at the core of that belief. All Christ-followers should ask themselves, "Where is Jesus in my theory?" when evaluating any issue.

Should we conclude that Jesus didn't care about this issue? Was He sending us a message through His example that there are more important things to worry about? Have we misread or overemphasized what the rest of the Bible teaches about so-called creation care?

We have to remember that Jesus came to earth in first-century Palestine where He ministered in a Jewish context. The people in Jesus' world were acutely aware of all the Hebrew laws and Scriptures that protected God's creation. The boys in Jesus' day memorized the story of Genesis and all Moses' laws at an early age. Some of the brighter ones would have memorized the Psalms, a book replete with natural imagery and content. Furthermore, first-century Palestine was largely an agrarian society in which sheer survival depended on sustainable practices and proper cultivation. Stewardship was assumed. So it isn't fair to fault Jesus for failing to offer answers to questions that the culture wasn't asking.

"The world of nature that we find in the Gospels is that of rural first-century Palestine," writes Alister McGrath. "It is a world where agrarian concerns—such as the growth of seeds, the fruitfulness of trees, imminent changes in weather, and the well-being of animals—were ever-present."[8]

Keeping these things in mind so that we evaluate our Lord fairly, we still find that His life and ministry powerfully bolster the divine plan for our planet. Jesus aligns with creation care in at least four ways.

Jesus Is the Creator-God

We first affirm that Jesus *is* God, and therefore, He is eternal. He created all that we see. As Paul tells us in Colossians 1, "He is the image of the invisible God, the firstborn over all creation. For by him all things were created: things in heaven and on earth, visible and invisible, whether thrones or powers or rulers or authorities; all things were created by him and for him" (Col. 1:15–16). The name for God in the creation account is plural, underscoring this idea. Because Jesus is the Creator-God, all the things we have demonstrated about God's heart for creation in the preceding chapters also apply to Jesus.

Because Jesus shares the identity of God, He "stands in the same relationship to creation as anything that is said of [God] in the Old Testament."[9] Therefore, it is totally appropriate for us to proclaim, "The earth is Jesus' and everything in it." And it is also appropriate to say that when we fail to care for creation properly, it is an affront to Jesus Christ Himself.

Jesus Entered Creation

"The rest of the world grows clearer, not dimmer, in the light of Christ," writes Philip Yancey. "God created matter; in Jesus, God joined it."[10] God paid creation the ultimate compliment when He entered it. Jesus Christ became a carbon-based life form, a human being. It is a lofty thought: the Creator became a part of creation. The same air we breathe entered His lungs. The same ground we trod bore food that satisfied His divine hunger. Prior to his public ministry, it is likely that Jesus worked with His hands as a carpenter in a highly agricultural society. Rather than hover above creation like a gypsy over a crystal ball, God entered creation and sent humanity a powerful message.

As Alister McGrath put it:

The Christian idea of the natural order as God's place of action and dwelling is intensified by the doctrine of incarnation, perhaps one of the most remarkable Christian ideas. In essence, the doctrine holds that God did not choose to remain in heaven, but entered into human history in the form of a human being. Rather than demanding that we ascend to God in order to be saved, God chose to enter into our world, to meet us there and to bring us home.... If God valued this world enough to enter into it, and dignify it with divine presence, then Christians ought to hold that place of habitation with appropriate respect.[11]

Although the incarnation of Christ has implications for the destiny of human souls, it also implies more. Jesus' mere presence on Earth affirms the value that God had already placed upon our planet. In other words, "Because Christ took on flesh, we believe matter matters."[12]

> Jesus' mere presence on Earth affirms the value that God had already placed upon our planet.

Jesus Taught with Creation

One of the things that made Jesus such a fascinating teacher was His ability to speak in simple, easy-to-understand terms. He had a knack for what writers and speakers sometimes call "putting the cookies on the lowest shelf." It is a paradox, really, that the most knowledgeable person who ever lived and who taught the most profound truths ever pondered, was so intellectually accessible that uneducated commoners clung to His sermons.

The tool that Jesus used most often to teach was the parable. Parables are self-contained, easy-to-understand stories that teach big ideas. Through parables, Jesus often taught about His kingdom in ways that engage the imagination. It is interesting that the elements Jesus chose to communicate these things were often natural. His stories were steeped in the imagery of nature—from seeds to animals, from the weather patterns to the rhythm of the seasons. Even Jesus' famous "I am" sayings in the Gospel of John are bathed in natural metaphors. In multiple places, Jesus likens Himself to bread, light, a vine, and a shepherd (John 6:35, 8:12, 10:11, 18:5).

I am not suggesting that Jesus embedded some deeper, mysterious environmental agenda in His parables or implying that we should read all of Jesus' teachings through green-tinted glasses. But we must affirm that when Jesus taught with nature or compared Himself to it, He was disclosing divine wisdom.

Without first understanding the divine plan, we don't properly understand some of Jesus' metaphors. Take Matthew 6:28, for example. In this passage, Jesus tells us that we shouldn't worry about how fashionably we dress because the native flowers are beautiful. This seems ridiculous unless we understand that implicit in Jesus' metaphor is an affirmation of the beauty of nature and God's provision as seen throughout the world. The divine plan informs the way we see Jesus' choice of language. Without the divine plan, we'd read over Jesus' description of the kingdom of God as a mustard seed that grows into a tree where birds can nest (Luke 13:18–19). But when we are informed by the divine plan, we conclude that Jesus draws on the world around us to teach us divine truth. In doing this, Jesus is making a powerful assumption about nature's ability to transmit information from and about God.[13]

Jesus Will Redeem Creation

Christian thinkers for some time have noted that when Adam sinned, it damaged humankind's relationships with God, creation, and us. Through Jesus, all of these things are being restored and redeemed. As Colossians 1 tells us, through Christ, "God was pleased to…reconcile to himself all things, whether things on earth or things in heaven, by making peace through his blood, shed on the cross" (Col. 1:19–20).

The prophet Isaiah foretold of a day when the chaos of creation would be brought back into order, when the lions and lambs would be led by children, and the earth would be filled with the knowledge of God (Isa. 11:6–9). The apostle Paul echoes this prophecy in Romans 8:21 when he writes, "The creation itself will be liberated from its bondage to decay." Indeed, one day Christ will return to fully restore and redeem all we see.

This does not mean we should sit idly by and wait for redemption. As Francis Schaeffer wrote:

On the basis of the fact that there is going to be total redemption in the future, not only of man but of all creation, the Christian who believes the Bible should be the man who—with God's help and in the power of the Holy Spirit—is treating nature now in the direction of the way nature will be then. It will not be perfect, but it must be substantial, or we have missed our calling…we should exhibit substantial healing here and now, between man and nature and nature and itself, as far as Christians can bring it to pass.[14]

The future does not provide an excuse for the present. Wars will continue until the Prince of Peace comes, but we must still pursue harmony now. Hunger and poverty will remain until the Bread of Life returns, but we must still care for those in need now. Sin will permeate this earth until the Spotless Lamb arrives, but we must preach forgiveness now. Our actions today should be driven by our knowledge of what is to come.

When asked where Jesus is in the divine plan for our planet, I confidently shout back, "Smack dab in the middle!" He stands above creation as its Inventor, He exists throughout creation as its Sustainer, He walked into creation as its Savior, and one day Jesus will return to creation as its Redeemer. "Since creation forms the platform of all God's mission in history, as well as being the final eschatological beneficiary of all God's redemptive intention, the centrality of Christ in that great mission of God within and for creation is clearly focused."[15]

There will always be snarky skeptics and cynics and people who have a vested interest in obscuring truth even when it is painfully obvious. Scripture teaches us with crystal clarity God loves this whole planet. He loves it so much, He assigned value to it. He loves it so much that He paused and took time to call it "good." He loves it so much that He has entered into a holy covenant with it. He loves it so much that He reveals parts of Himself through it. He loves it so much that He asked us to take good care of it until He returns to redeem it. I've called it *the divine plan for our planet*, and it compels me to think differently about the world and its citizens.

PLAN POINT: In order to hold to the divine plan with confidence, we must be able to answer the skeptics and cynics and other Christian believers clearly and biblically.

OUR ASSIGNMENT IN GOD'S WORLD

8

FACING THE FACTS

THE waiting room in my doctor's office has only eight chairs, and somehow mine always seems to be the last one emptied. I've gotten used to waiting a long time when I go in for a check-up so I always try to show up a bit late. This day, for some reason, I arrived early. I checked in with the mysterious woman behind the sliding glass window and tried to select a seat away from the coughing adolescents. I foolishly made the appointment at lunchtime, and my hunger was breeding regret. I couldn't even find the bowl of children's lollipops that come standard with most waiting rooms.

Ten minutes.

Twenty.

Thirty.

My stomach was beginning to get angry, and I didn't blame it. I was starving. Who did my doctor think he was to make me skip lunch like this? I snatched up a copy of *National Geographic* to get my mind off this injustice, and the first article I came to was titled "Poor Haitians Resort to Eating Dirt." I felt ashamed as I read.

Charlene Dumas is a typical sixteen-year-old pregnant woman living in Cité Soleil, Haiti, who is so desperately hungry that she has resorted to eating cakes made of vegetable shortening and dirt. Because the soil in Haiti is so badly damaged, the land is unable to produce enough food for the people to survive. It has gotten so bad that the United Nations Food and Agriculture Agency has declared a state of emergency there. In desperation, many Haitians are driven to feast on dirt patties, which often contain deadly parasites and toxins.

Have you ever been so hungry you sarcastically remark that you'd eat almost anything? When Haitians say it, they mean it. "When my mother does not cook anything, I have to eat them three times a day," Charlene says.[1]

Haiti's environmental situation is dire, but that isn't the only country fighting environmental degradation. More than 250 million people living in developing countries are struggling because of arable land loss resulting from human-induced erosion and desertification. Each year, 1,374 square miles of land become desert.[2] In 1991, the International Soil Reference and Information Centre conducted the most comprehensive study of soil globally and found that 7.5 million square miles of soil have been destroyed. That's roughly the size of Canada and the United States combined.[3]

Environmental problems are real, and they don't exist only in the quiet corners of the third world. Every country on Earth has its own environmental problems that need

> Environmental problems are real, and they don't exist only in the quiet corners of the third world.

addressing. But before we address anything, we have to recognize that a problem exists.

THE DEVIL IN THE DETAILS

Some think environmental problems are overblown. They debate rather than seek solutions, and their skepticism often serves as insulation from reality. In order to bring progress to a shuddering halt, one doesn't have to disprove but merely cast doubt. I've spent much time with people like this, and I am convinced that their problem isn't a lack of concern, but rather a lack of education. They exemplify Montaigne's axiom, which declares, "Nothing is so firmly believed as what we least know." Today, it seems everyone thinks they are an expert on everything.

When the uninformed forcibly face the environmental facts, they are silenced. As Daniel Patrick Moynihan once said, "Everyone is entitled to his own opinion, but not to his own facts." Our water, air, land, and wildlife are all suffering at the hands of those whom God has assigned to protect them. We can disagree on what should be done, but it is clear that something must be done and that we must address ecological crises if we want to live in step with the divine plan.

Land

Poor soil fertility and quality are two of the most daunting environmental crises facing humanity. Much of the time, the soil is ruined by farmers or gatherers who don't know better or who *do* know better but either don't care or are so desperate to feed their families that they exhaust the soil. Sometimes, the fault falls on greedy developers looking to make a buck and other times it falls on oppressive governments.

"Agriculture has too often involved an insupportable abuse and waste of soil, ever since the first farmers took away the soil-saving cover and roots of perennial plants. Civilizations have destroyed themselves by destroying their farmland," write Wes Jackson and Wendell Berry. "This irremediable loss, never enough noticed, has been made worse by the huge monocultures and continuous soil-exposure of the agriculture we now practice."[4]

Whether caused by farmers, developers, or others, land degradation is not a problem that we can afford to ignore and hope that it goes away. When soil goes bad, the land is unable to produce food, and when food is absent, people die. Bad soil equals poor agriculture and poor health. In many places, including the great cities of North America, the soil has been contaminated with chemicals and carcinogens and in other places, the life-giving topsoil has been completely obliterated. Additionally, we're leveling the world's forests quicker than Paul Bunyan. Though God wants us to protect our land, we keep treating it like dirt.

- About half of Earth's tropical and temperate forests have already been destroyed.[5]
- Approximately twenty-five hectares of natural forests—the size of thirty-six football fields—are lost every minute.[6]
- Our tropical rain forests are home to some of God's most unique creatures and rarest medicines, but humans destroy about twenty-five million acres annually. That is an area roughly the size of the state of Indiana each year.[7]

- According to the U.S. Department of Agriculture's Natural Resources Conservation Service, 33 percent of global land surface is experiencing desertification as a result of erosion, overgrazing, and a changing climate. This affects more than one billion people, half of whom live in Africa.[8]

Our planet's environmental problems stretch well beyond soil. To determine our role in the divine plan accurately, we have to begin facing the brutal environmental facts.

Water

In the beginning, there were more than 300 million trillion gallons of water on Planet Earth. Today, there are still more than 300 million trillion gallons. Water is a unique natural resource in that it is never depleted. But almost all of that is salty seawater, unpotable for most plants, animals, and people. Of the small fraction of fresh water available for use, our actions have led to contamination or a diversion from where it is most needed.[9] We have created a global clean water crisis, and as the saying goes, you never know the worth of water until the well runs dry.

- According to the World Water Council, more than 1.1 billion people lack access to safe drinking water, 3.4 million people die every year from preventable, water-related diseases, and thirty-nine hundred children die every day from water-borne diseases.[10]
- The World Health Organization estimates that 1.8 million people die each year from diarrheal disease. Almost 90 percent of these deaths are a result of unclean

drinking water and poor sanitation. Most deaths occur among children in developing countries.[11]

- Coral reefs are some of the most biologically diverse and productive systems found anywhere on Earth. According to the World Resources Institute, approximately 25 percent of the coral reefs on Earth have already disappeared. It is estimated that two-thirds of all reefs are now at risk, due to a combination of water pollution, thermal stress from warming oceans, and changing ocean chemistry.[12]

- Of the nineteen countries globally currently classified as water-stressed, more are in Africa than any other region.[13]

- Worldwide, more than 700 million people are directly dependent upon fisheries for food. Approximately 30 percent of the world's fisheries have collapsed or are near collapse as a result of overfishing.[14]

Air

Some things in life are unavoidable. Breathing in the air around you is one of them. Children and the poor don't have a choice regarding air quality, and even people around the globe who do have choices about where they live are breathing in harmful particles, smoke, and airborne toxins every day. As Robert Orben once quipped, "There's so much pollution in the air now that if it weren't for our lungs, there'd be no place to put it all." One can't help but wonder what God thinks about the "air of our ways."

- The World Health Organization reports that more than two million people die annually from air pollution. Most deaths recorded are in poor countries.[15]

- According to the United Nations Environment Programme, more than one billion people are exposed to dangerous outdoor air pollution every year.[16]

- Indoor air pollution, much of it from using unimproved cook stoves that burn wood, charcoal, and even animal dung, is responsible for one in twenty deaths in most affected countries, according to the World Health Organization.[17]

- As air pollution has increased, asthma cases have increased by more than 60 percent since 1980. One out of every three asthma victims is a child.[18]

- According to the National Oceanic and Atmospheric Administration, global toxic emissions, including carbon dioxide, methane, chlorofluorocarbons (CFCs), and nitrous oxide, have continued to rise for more than fifty years. Many experts believe this is directly responsible for recent changes in the earth's climate. Even if you disagree with the concept of climate change, it should be obvious that pumping massive amounts of toxic gases into the air is a bad thing.[19]

Wildlife

God has blessed us with incredible wildlife. These populations are robust in the face of incredible disturbances and disasters, but humanity can still be a daunting and destructive force. As a result of human actions, the very creatures that Adam carefully named are disappearing from the face of our planet. Contrary to popular wisdom, hunting is not the primary reason for declines in animal populations; the main threat is habitat loss from urban expansion and the conversion of natural systems to agriculture.

- Seventy percent of the world's coastal fish stocks are overexploited or collapsed.[20]

- We are experiencing extinction rates well over one thousand times higher than the natural extinction rate. Although the numbers vary, experts agree that we are facing a massive loss of biodiversity.[21]

- The Living Planet Index, which tracks almost four thousand wildlife populations, shows a 27 percent fall in population trends since 1970.[22]

- More than 20 percent of the world's freshwater species have become extinct, threatened, or endangered in recent decades.[23]

- According to the scientific journal *Nature*, 90 percent of the world's "big fish" are gone.[24]

- One in eight birds, one in four mammals, one in three amphibians, and almost half of freshwater turtles are threatened with extinction.[25]

Stop for a minute and meditate on these facts—snapshots of the devastation occurring around the globe. People dying with parched lips and empty stomachs. Children breathing in grey air and coughing up blood. Animals vanishing from the face of the earth. Dense forests, which have been here for centuries, wiped from existence.

Is this the "glory" that the psalmist sang about? Is this what the Scripture's authors call "the works of the Lord"? Are our actions lining up with all the things we've learned about God's heart?

> Our world is so far outside of the divine plan, we need to stop debating and start acting to restore God's vision for this world.

In *Approaching Hoofbeats*, Billy Graham wrote, "The growing possibility of our destroying ourselves and the world with our own neglect and excess is tragic and very real." Although I don't believe that human beings are on the brink of extinction, I do believe that many of our problems are grave. We are doing a poor job of caring for the planet God loves, of worshiping and obeying the One who created everything. Our world is so far outside of the divine plan, we need to stop debating and start acting to restore God's vision for this world from one end of the globe to the other.

IGNORANCE IS BLISS, BUT NOT ALWAYS BEST

If I live a thousand years, I'll never forget the last few months of my grandfather's life. "Papa" was a grizzly bear of a man. A typical Old South man—tough, hardworking, a Great Depression survivor who never developed aspirations for life's finer things. He was as satisfied riding his rusty red lawnmower as others might be inside a brand-new BMW.

I had a special place in Papa's heart, I think. Not that he loved me any more than his other grandkids, but he and I seemed to have a unique relationship. The day I found out that his lung cancer had spread to his lymph nodes, I felt as if I had been punched in the stomach. I guess I thought he'd get well because, in my mind, he would always be around. At that moment, I knew better.

My brother and I were with him the night he died. He was in a hospital room hooked up to all kinds of machines. We sat in silence. The doctor had given him several more months to live, so if I had known he wouldn't be alive the next day I would have stayed longer. I should have known, though, because when we got up to go home, he grabbed just enough air to beg, "Please don't leave." The gruff exterior of this Southern giant had fallen off. How could I say no? My brother and I stayed for a few more minutes before leaving, and my Papa passed that night. No one could have predicted that would be our last time together on Earth.

More than a half century before my Papa passed away, Douglas Fairbanks suffered from a heart attack in 1939. After he woke up, he decided that he felt well and went back to bed. He died shortly after hitting the pillow. He was fifty-six. His last words before heading back to sleep were, "I've never felt better."[26]

Six years later, Franklin D. Roosevelt was visiting one of his favorite retreats when he died of a cerebral hemorrhage. While posing for a portrait, President Roosevelt spoke his last words: "I have a terrific headache."

As these stories illustrate, we don't know when we will die. The old saying says "Ignorance is bliss." We live in perpetual ignorance. No one knows know if tomorrow will bring job loss or a lifestyle-changing raise, if Mr. or Mrs. Right will come strolling through the next open door or a longtime spouse will decide one day that he or she has "fallen out of love." No one knows if the stock market will soar over the next year or crash and leave us all penniless.

Even if it were possible, most of us wouldn't want to know the future. A measure of freedom comes with not knowing. Once we receive facts, we become responsible for how we respond to that knowledge.

I was more comfortable before I knew these alarming statistics. I was more carefree before I knew where our world was headed and what future realities were quickly approaching. Once I had the information, I felt I should care. I know God does.

Before it got cancelled, one of my favorite shows on television was called *Early Edition.* The plot was simple yet intriguing. Each day, Gary Hobson receives a copy of the *Chicago Sun-Times* on his doorstep. He doesn't know where the newspaper comes from or who puts it there or why an orange cat is always sitting beside it. If that isn't strange enough, the newspaper is always the next day's edition and filled with tragedy that hasn't even happened yet. So Gary spends every day righting wrongs, saving lives, and changing destiny.

What would you do if you got tomorrow's paper today? Would you flip to the obituaries and make sure you weren't there? Would you look up the sports scores and call your bookie? Or would you pretend you never saw it and live your life in ignorance? I bet many of us—myself included—would think long and hard about the last option. Most of us wouldn't want the responsibility.

The Bible teaches that as knowledge increases, responsibility also increases. In John 9:41, Jesus says, "If you were blind, you would not be guilty of sin; but now that you claim you can see, your guilt remains." And James 4:17 teaches, "Anyone, then, who knows the good he ought to do and doesn't do it, sins." (See also John 15:22–24; Luke 12:47–48, Luke 21:1–4; 2 Pet. 2:21.) We know from Scripture what God expects from us with regard to the creation. The question becomes whether or not we will respond to that.

We are faced with a choice. We must choose either to ignore the state of our planet or to act. If we fail to act, knowing what God desires from us, we are sinning and the problems will only get worse. When I was growing up, my mother used to tell me, "If you keep doing the same things the same way, you shouldn't expect different results."

If we choose to get involved in these issues, united around God's plan, perhaps we will preserve God's handiwork, save lives, and magnify our Maker.

9

THE ENEMY IN US ALL

I love cartoons. Whether it's an old school *Tom and Jerry* short or the latest DreamWorks flick, I'll come running like a kindergartner on Christmas morning. I've always been fascinated by them, and when I was a child, I would try to draw cartoons during church's more boring moments. You don't think of cartoonists as being particularly deep thinkers, but one cartoonist—Walt Kelly—was particularly profound.

Kelly was a cartoonist during the mid-twentieth century. For several years, Kelly worked for Walt Disney Productions where he contributed to such animated classics as *Snow White and the Seven Dwarfs*, *Dumbo*, and *Fantasia*. He is most well known for *Pogo*, a comic strip centering on a wily pack of animals living in Georgia's Okefenokee Swamp. The strip first appeared in the 1940s and continued to run well after Kelly's death in 1973.

One of the things that made *Pogo* so famous was that the comic strip had teeth. Kelly, a liberal humanist in an era when being a liberal humanist wasn't cool, often used the strip as a medium to communicate his political and social views through lighthearted satire. His effectiveness in this area allowed him to speak into culture in ways uncommon for a cartoonist in that day. One of his most famous quotes appeared on a poster for Earth Day in 1970: "We have met the enemy, and he is us."[1]

I stumbled across Kelly's poster while browsing the Internet one day, and I came to a painful conclusion. Kelly might as well have been making that poster for Americans in 2010. We currently consume more and waste more than any group of people living at any time since the world began. What's worse, most of us don't even realize it.

Environmentally speaking, our heads are in the clouds. We look around our suburban fortresses and see no devastation. We walk our dogs through landscaped parks. We wake up and breathe in air that seems fresh enough. We take a swig of clean, clear water straight out of the faucet without fear of a midday visit from Montezuma. Because we have been so financially blessed, most of us purchase the things we want, use them for a while, and then throw them away without worrying about where they'll end up.

Most of us live oblivious to any environmental crises, so Americans rest easy. Unfortunately, our solace is like drinking rum in a snowstorm. We feel warm, but the warmth isn't real. Ecological problems are bubbling up both at home and abroad. America has its share of environmental problems, and though many of them are localized to poorer neighborhoods and forgotten

> People around the globe pay for the unsustainable lifestyles that Americans consider normal.

places, others intensely affect our children and us. Worse still, other people around the globe pay for the unsustainable life-styles that Americans consider normal as we shift the burden to other nations' citizens and export our way of life. As we realize the American dream, much of the rest of the world is waking up to environmental nightmares.

At the May 7, 2001, White House daily press briefing, Ari Fleischer, White House spokesperson for President George W. Bush, was asked a tough environmental question: "Does the president believe that, given the amount of energy Americans consume per capita—how much it exceeds any other citizens in any other country in the world—does the president believe we need to correct our lifestyles to address the energy problem?"

Without hesitation, Fleischer snapped back, "That's a big no. The president believes that it's an American way of life, and that it should be the goal of policy makers to protect the American way of life. The American way of life is a blessed one."[2]

In the middle of that train-wreck answer, Fleischer managed to give us a gem of truth. Overconsumption of energy, and virtually every resource imaginable, has become "the American way of life." What's worse is that Americans are the only ones who don't seem to realize it.

When it comes to being green, the international community largely sees us as people with a whole lot of style but not nearly enough substance. The sentiment prompted automobile giant Daimler to advertise its eco-friendly "forfour" smart car on a billboard in South Africa with the slogan, "German engineering, Swiss innovation, American nothing."[3]

If you want an unforgettable picture of the true cost of the American way of life, visit the Appalachian Mountains in West Virginia, Kentucky, and Tennessee. In those regions, coal companies wreak havoc on the land God loves, and innocent people and communities pay the price.

Imagine walking up to a mountain in this region. It is a mountain that the Creator Himself shaped, it is covered with soil and trees and animals that God loves. Then imagine cutting every tree from the native forest that has inhabited this space for more than a hundred years. Once it is completely bald, imagine stuffing it with massive explosive charges and blasting it to smithereens. If that weren't reprehensible enough, imagine taking all of the dirt that you removed—which has now been contaminated with toxic waste—and dumping it into the rivers and their headwaters, often burying them completely. When the families and communities of this land cry out because they are forced to breathe in all of the dust, navigate the unstable slopes, and drink polluted well water, you simply ignore them. When the lifelong residents beg you to stop because they can't bear to watch you obliterate the land their grandfathers hunted on, you flash your government-issued permit and shoo them away.

In Appalachia, where many of our nation's poorest people live, this is exactly what is going on every day. Over the past twenty years, five hundred square miles of West Virginia have been "stripped" into desert land. More than three hundred thousand acres of this state have now received surface mining permits, and less than 1 percent of the mined land is ever reused for any development purpose whatsoever.[4]

The poor people of this land are the victims of injustice and greed, the land that God loves is being pillaged, and most Americans aren't doing a thing. The coal is being used to feed our energy addiction.

Some lawmakers, including Christian advocacy groups with a penchant for defending big corporations, have turned a blind eye to this atrocity. They claim that strip mining is good for the economy and that people aren't really suffering that badly. But the victims of the Buffalo Creek disaster would plead otherwise. This 1972 flood was the worst in history and was caused by a dam that burst as a result of strip mining. Approximately 138 million gallons of black wastewater from the Buffalo Creek Coal Company flooded the narrow hollow, spoiling the land, killing 125 people, and leaving thousands homeless.[5]

When I first saw the devastation caused by mountaintop removal, my initial reaction was silence. I could not believe my eyes. *Surely this isn't happening in America*, I thought. *Maybe in a developing country with a corrupt government, but not here.* Matthew Sleeth, a former emergency room doctor and author of *Serve God, Save the Planet*, described it with language from his medical background: rape.[6] I have to agree with him. When my eyes saw this, I could sense the land and its Maker don't want this. But humans are doing it anyway. My indignation grew when I spoke with affected residents who choked back tears as they shared stories.

What was once breathtaking country that spoke volumes about God's beauty and majesty and provision now looks like a travel guide for Kansas. The mountains, which should be declaring God's glory, are being devoured, divorced from the divine plan. Although wonderful organizations like

Restoring Eden and Christians for the Mountains are making progress in this fight, more must be done.

It doesn't stop with Appalachia. On the other coast, we have created an equally dire situation. It is called the "North Pacific Gyre" or the "great Pacific garbage patch." It is a floating soup of trash almost twice the size of Texas that is stewing in the middle of the North Pacific Ocean. According to marine biologists and oceanographers, this pottage consists of 80 percent plastics and could weigh more than 100 million tons. The vast majority of this trash is from onshore sources and has been dumped by consumers and industries.[7]

This floating mass of discarded water bottles, toothbrushes, shopping bags, shampoo bottles, and bottle caps wreaks havoc on marine life. Animals become entangled and die, and as the trash breaks down, fish and birds ingest it.[8]

I ask myself what God thinks about us trashing His creation with our selfish, wasteful lifestyles. The first half of this book is the answer. These tragedies undoubtedly grieve the heart of God. Calamities like these are all around us.

- According to the 2005 report by the American Lung Association, 55 percent of Americans live in areas with unhealthy levels of ozone or particle pollution. The areas with the highest concentration of pollution are—you guessed it—the poorest urban neighborhoods.[9]

- Almost half of America's lakes and rivers are too polluted for swimming or aquatic life. If you took your son or daughter fishing in these lakes, you wouldn't be allowed to eat your catch because it would contain dangerous levels of toxic chemicals.[10] If you live near a body of water, ask yourself if you would eat the fish swimming in there or drink even a drop from it.

- The Mississippi River drains almost half of the continental United States. It is one of the most precious environmental resources Americans possess. Yet it carries approximately 1.5 million metric tons of nitrogen pollution into the Gulf of Mexico every year. The "dead zone" this produces in the gulf is roughly the size of Massachusetts.[11]

- Every year, American factories churn out three million tons of toxic chemicals into the surrounding environment.[12]

- Americans are, by far, the number-one producers of garbage on the planet. Americans produce about double the amount of waste the rest of the world averages. We discard 4.5 pounds of garbage per day, which would fill sixty-three thousand garbage trucks.[13]

- Much of the waste that could be recycled isn't. Of the waste that is thrown away, a large portion is incinerated, which releases harmful gases into the atmosphere, and the rest is placed in landfills to decompose. For example, Americans generate 30 billion foam cups each year, which take hundreds of years to decompose.[14]

Just because you don't see it doesn't mean it isn't there. Environmental problems are cloaked for many of us, but they are present and closer than we think. Our lifestyles produce grey skylines, grimy water, and mountains of toxic waste.

The wonderful things about America should not be overlooked. We are a generous, charitable nation and the greatest defenders of freedom in history. I wouldn't live anywhere else. Yet Americans are the most consumerist and wasteful people in the world, and our sins spill onto other nations and people groups.

American lifestyles affect the international community. We shift the burden of our lifestyles to others. For example, according to the Central Intelligence Agency, America consumes more than 20.6 million barrels of oil daily. The next highest consumer is China, which consumes about a third of that amount despite a greater population.[15] This is excessive consumption, but the problem runs deeper. As we purchase oil, we fund Organization of Petroleum Exporting Countries (OPEC) like Iran, Libya, and Saudi Arabia whose governments outlaw Christianity, oppress women, and often sponsor terrorism. "Through our energy purchases we are funding both sides of the war on terror," writes Thomas Friedman. "I cannot think of anything more stupid."[16]

Our lifestyles fund injustice.

Another example is an American staple—paper. Though America represents only 5 percent of the world's population, we consume approximately 33 percent of the world's paper products.[17] The massive amount of paper we consume comes largely from South American countries where pristine rain forests once thrived. Those natural greeneries are being demolished. From August 2007 to July 2008, approximately twelve thousand square kilometers of the Brazilian Amazon were deforested. That's an area of land roughly the size of

Jamaica denuded in one year.[18] Between 1990 and 2005, 21 percent of the total forest cover in Ecuador was lost.[19]

In places that are closer to home and cheaper to import, the situation is even worse. Little natural forest cover remains in the Caribbean, and entire Central American forests in some countries have been completely wiped out. Between 1990 and 2005, 20 percent of the forest cover in Nicaragua and El Salvador, 17 percent of the forest cover in Guatemala, and a whopping 37 percent of all forest cover in Honduras was demolished.[20]

Deforestation occurs for a number of reasons from clearing land for settlements and agriculture to producing timber. However, the demand for pulp and paper production is an enormous factor.

Brazilians, Ecuadorians, Hondurans—our global neighbors—all depend on the natural resources of their countries. This is increasingly true for those who don't have the financial resources to cope with environmental problems. Environmental opponents often mention the benefits to foreign economies that are dependent on cash for exporting paper products to the United States. However, these forestlands have often been wrested from the indigenous people. Timber companies are frequently given illegal permits by corrupt governments. Ordinary people in exporting countries often benefit little from selling their patrimony to produce more paper for you and me. Americans overconsume paper while people elsewhere pay the price. Our consumption creates social and economic instability that provokes such atrocities as disease and war.

"The only question is whether [environmental problems] will be resolved in pleasant ways of our choice, or in unpleasant ways not of our choice, such as warfare, genocide, starvation, disease epidemics, and collapse of societies," writes Jared Diamond in his book *Collapse: How Societies Choose to Succeed or Fail*. "While all of those grim phenomena have been endemic to humanity throughout our history, their frequency increases with environmental degradation, population pressure, and the resulting poverty and instability."[21]

Diamond hints at a stark truth: if current trends persist, we should expect the situation to get much worse. Perhaps the two biggest trends at play here are the global population boom and the global prosperity boom. It's no secret that population rates have been skyrocketing in recent years. It took the human race thousands of years to reach one billion inhabitants. In the past forty to forty-five years, the world's population has doubled.[22] Almost seven billion people currently inhabit Earth, and that number is rising rapidly. Experts predict that within the next fifty years, the world will grow by another 50 to 60 percent.[23] Each new person means another mouth to feed, another person who is consuming resources and creating waste.

This has led many enviro groups to support population control platforms, which often include supporting abortions. While we should be aware of population growth, such measures are immoral and must be rejected.

As population rises, so does prosperity. As Thomas Friedman extensively describes in *The World Is Flat*, the global middle class is swelling. Experts say that the world's economy will double in size in only fourteen years.[24]

> If current trends persist, we should expect the situation to get much worse.

On a recent flight to Africa to work with an orphanage and do health education, I sat next to a woman from Kenya whose life was indistinguishable from those in middle-class America of similar age. Her kids were in private schools. She wore attractive but not outlandish jewelry. She spoke clear English and was reading a book by a popular American pastor that I often see preaching on television. The media portrayal of an African woman as a poor rural villager living life on the economic fringes is a stereotype. It isn't as true as it once was. Things are leveling off in many places. This doesn't mean that poverty is gone, but the middle class is definitely swelling. (To be fair, some statistics point out that the total number of poor people has fallen. But there is no sign that poverty is actually disappearing.) Many of our current problems exist at the intersection of population and prosperity.

THE NEED FOR REINVENTION

Americans have exerted significant influence over the prosperity boom. We export Americanism globally through entertainment, sodas, foods, and the international promotion of the American Dream. I have been fortunate to travel much of the globe—Mexico, Canada, South America, Africa, Western Europe, and the Middle East—and I remain astonished at how people everywhere I go fanatically envy American consumption.

As Thomas Friedman says, "Americans are popping up all over now—from Doha to Dalian and from Calcutta to Casablanca to Cairo, moving into American-style living spaces, buying American-style cars, eating American-style fast food, and creating American levels of garbage. The planet has never seen so many Americans."[25] If everyone on Earth actually consumed resources the way Americans do, experts estimate that it would take several Planet Earths just to sustain life.[26]

The growing worldwide population and increasing global middle class that seeks American "consumption" is creating a perfect storm of ecological crises. America needs to lead the world to make positive changes, but we can't even control our own habits. The Chinese have the world's fastest growing economy and 1.3 billion citizens. They are massive consumers and are way above the world's average consumption rate. Yet the per capita consumption rates in China still remain less than a tenth of those of the United States.[27]

The "American way" is broken and needs to be reinvented. We have to have the best of everything in America, but we rarely consider how this affects our global neighbors. As one environmental expert said of our current situation, "We are either going to be losers or heroes—there's no room for anything in between."[28] Either way, the world will take note of our response.

> The "American way" is broken and needs to be reinvented.

When I reflect on the forests being lost, the societies destabilized, and the oppressive dictatorships being funded by our wasteful materialism and contrast all that to the divine plan, my heart grieves. It reminds me of the words of the prophet Ezekiel: "Is it not enough for you to feed on the good pasture? Must you also trample the rest of the pasture with your feet? Is it not enough for you to drink clear water? Must you also muddy the rest with your feet?" (Ezek. 34:18).

The world needs Americans to become the heroes that God has empowered us to be.

10

DO THESE JEANS MAKE MY LANDFILL LOOK FAT?

I have never been one to wake up before the sun to take advantage of all the retail insanity on the day after Thanksgiving. I question the mental stability of such people. After stuffing my face on Thanksgiving, the last thing I want to do is fight crowds and stand in lines. I'd rather stay home to snack on leftovers and ask forgiveness for the previous day's gluttony. I'll never forget the horror I felt on that Friday morning in 2008 when I heard that a worker at Wal-Mart had been trampled to death by out-of-control shoppers.

Jdimytai Damour was a thirty-four-year-old Haitian immigrant who took a job at Wal-Mart as a seasonal employee after working in the construction industry. He was tall, healthy, and a resident of Queens, New York. His favorite novelist was Donald Goines.

Damour and his family weren't strangers to violence and tragedy. *Traveler's Digest* named Haiti one of the world's most dangerous destinations.[1] Damour had no idea that he was facing death when Wal-Mart's doors opened in Valley Stream, New York, on November 28, 2008.

At 4:55 a.m., on the infamous shopping day known as Black Friday, tension was building outside the Wal-Mart. More than two thousand shoppers had gathered to be the first inside to take advantage of the many advertised sales. People were banging their fists and shoppers were screaming as glass shattered and doors swung open just before the 5 a.m. opening. That's when Damour was helplessly thrown backwards onto the black linoleum floor and trampled to death by the shrieking mob madly searching for plasma TVs and digital cameras.

Detective Lt. Michael Fleming later told the *New York Times* that the scene was "utter chaos." Kimberly Cribbs, a local resident who witnessed the tragedy, remarked that the crowd acted like "savages." They and others stood there as other employees and police officers tried to rescue Damour, to no avail. The innocent immigrant was dead. Perhaps most appalling was shoppers' behavior as the store was being cleared. "When they were saying they had to leave, that an employee got killed, people were yelling, 'I've been in line since yesterday morning,'" Ms. Cribbs told the Associated Press. "They kept shopping."[2]

WE, THE CULPRITS

I am reminded of a Bob Dylan song, "Who Killed Davey Moore?" about a boxer who died of injuries from a fight in 1963. The song repeatedly asks who is responsible for the boxer's death and in each verse, everyone denies fault—the referee, the bloodthirsty crowd, his manager, the bookies, and Davey's opponent. No one seems to be responsible for the boxer's death.

Who is responsible for the death of Jdimytai Damour? Was it the mob that actually did the trampling, the people who saw what was going on but were too afraid to intervene, the Wal-Mart executives who set the ridiculously low prices that attracted these shoppers, or the store managers who failed to prepare a more organized plan for the store's opening? Cases have been made for all of these, and none are totally innocent.

We all have blood on our hands. We are all culpable. The weight of trampling shoppers crushed Damour. Consumerism, greed, indifference killed him. Damour's death was more than a failure to keep order; it was a failure of values by an every-man-for-himself society that has made greed our god.

Shameless consumerism drives life in America. We have permitted a culture that rushes through the graceful holiday of Thanksgiving to celebrate the High Holy Day of Mindless Consumerism.[3] This comes at a high price, not merely measured in graphs, charts, gross domestic products, and dissertations by students at Harvard Business School. It is paid for with the natural resources that we have to harvest to feed our insane consumer habits. It is paid for with the useless land destruction and results in the mountainous piles of waste we produce. And on November 28, 2008, in one neighborhood's local Wal-Mart, the ultimate price

We often fail to connect consumerism to creation's woes, but when you find one, the other is usually not far away.

was paid with the loss of God's greatest creation—human life. We often fail to connect consumerism to creation's woes, but when you find one, the other is usually not far away.

OUR NATIONAL DISEASE

An attractive, well-dressed female sits in a doctor's office nervously twiddling her thumbs waiting for a diagnosis. "Nothing physically is wrong with you," the doctor says.

"What? That can't be," the patient says incredulously. "I feel so terrible. I feel bloated, sluggish, and worthless, but I should feel great. After all, I have a giant new house, a brand-new car, an expensive wardrobe, and a job that pays me a ridiculous wad of cash. Yet I'm miserable. Can't you just give me a pill to make it go away?"

The doctor shakes his head. "Unfortunately, I can't. No pill exists for your disease," he says.

"My *disease?* What do I have?" she asks in a panic.

"Affluenza," he answers grimly. "An epidemic has broken out. It can be cured but the treatment is long and painful."[4]

Affluenza is a term that was coined in a film and later a book by the same name. The authors define Affluenza as "a painful, contagious, socially-transmitted condition of overload, debt, anxiety, and waste resulting from the dogged pursuit of more."[5] It afflicts every American, including good ol' Christian Americans—this author among them—in one way or another.

Americans are a charitable people, but what we give away is not quite as astounding when seen in proportion to what we keep. (What made the widow's mite so powerful was not that she gave much but that she gave sacrificially relative to what she had.) According to the U.S. Census Bureau, Americans spend as much on automobile maintenance as we do on religious and welfare activities. About 30 percent of Americans purchase Christmas presents for their pets; only 11 percent buy them for their neighbors.[6] The mark of our society is envy more than charity. An ad for the jewelry designer David Yurman pictures insanely expensive trinkets and says: "There's that old, familiar feeling again: insatiable want."[7]

Our relentless pursuit of money has been accompanied by myriad problems. American marriages disintegrate at astronomical rates. One of the most common reasons for divorce is financial pressure. Americans usually promise to stick with their partners for richer or poorer, but in the age of Affluenza, poorer is no longer an option.

Affluenza is also infecting the family, another strained institution. Rather than spend time with those we love, Americans put in more hours on the job. According to a recent United Nations study, American workers toil more hours annually than the labor force of any other industrialized nation.[8] "The pressure that materialism is bringing to bear on the American family today is woefully underestimated, but it is critically important," argues Glenn Stanton, former policy analyst for Focus on the Family.

This national disease wreaks havoc on God's green earth. The previous chapter related that Americans consume more than any other nation and create unfathomable waste. One American, for example, consumes about as much as 32 Kenyans.[9] Each year, Americans toss 250 million pounds of pizza boxes, tires, designer shoes, diapers, beer bottles, couches, phone books, and half-eaten burritos into land-fills.[10] We throw away roughly 4.5 million pounds of carpet alone.[11]

Americans would do well to heed the words of the apostle Paul:

For we brought nothing into the world, and we can take nothing out of it. But if we have food and cloth-ing, we will be content with that. People who want to get rich fall into temptation and a trap and into many foolish and harmful desires that plunge men into ruin and destruction. For the love of money is a root of all kinds of evil. Some people, eager for money, have wan-dered from the faith and pierced themselves with many griefs. (1 Timothy 6:7-10)

The Bible's teachings on greed and material idolatry are part of the reason that I dreaded addressing this particular issue. I wrestle with Affluenza many days and lose more often than not. Like most Americans, I struggle with sinful consumerism and materialism. I enjoy material things. I live in a big house (by global standards) and drive a cur-rent model car. I wear nice clothes, many of which I bought from designer stores in a mega-mall. When I see how my materialism plays out in society, I feel the most awful guilt. Material things

> The human tendency to pursue more and better is impossible to reconcile with the divine plan.

are not themselves inherently evil, but my unbridled desires are. My tendency to pursue more and better is impossible to reconcile with the divine plan.

A few months ago, I was speaking with an acquaintance who began teaching at a religious university. After settling into his new office, he decided he needed to buy an automobile. He was naturally looking for a small economy car that got good gas mileage. Standing in the faculty lounge one afternoon, he was mentioning the models he was interested in purchasing to some other professors. One of his colleagues pulled him aside and said, "In America, a professor wouldn't drive a car like that. You should really look into a Lincoln or something more appropriate." The comment angered and confused him. My friend replied with the first thing that came to mind: "I am purchasing an automobile to get me from point A to point B—not to tell everyone how much money I have."

The encounter makes a powerful point. We must constantly consider our motives. Before you hand your credit card to a cashier or reach for an item on a shelf, ask yourself *why* you are purchasing that particular item. Are your desires for that object driven by people's perceptions of you? Will this purchase serve a real purpose in your life or is it another trinket you'll simply accumulate? Driving a nice car doesn't make you self-absorbed any more than driving a beat-up clunker makes you self-effacing. In America, we buy things every day that nobody needs. The Scriptures remind us that we can't take any of these things with us into the afterlife. Instead of seeking more and better things, let's strive to be more content with what we have and cautious about what we buy.

As a New Year's resolution last year, I decided to begin cutting excess out of my life. I started by significantly reducing red meat and pork in my diet. I had no idea how difficult this would be, especially given my culture. We love our barbeque in the South. Ribs and pulled pork slathered in a rich, sweet-mesquite barbeque sauce are an essential part of any good Southern celebration. Things get worse at the tailgate during football season Saturdays. But I know that, unfortunately, the food we eat has an effect on the world around us. God cares about what we eat.

Americans eat about eight ounces of meat daily per person, roughly twice the global average.[12] Our meat addiction doesn't sound too serious until you consider the impact our current systems are having on the soil, God's creatures, the environment, and us. In America, all or most of the meat in your local supermarket comes from "factory farms," in which large stocks of chickens, pigs, cows, and other animals are crammed into confined spaces for the duration of their lives. The industrial practice gets its name from the factory-like practices by which animals are processed like simple material products.

The area surrounding Raleigh, North Carolina, where I lived during seminary, is one of the premier regions for factory farming in the United States. For two years, whenever I flew into Raleigh-Durham International Airport, I would peer out my oval window at long, windowless boxes that looked like large storage facilities. Later I discovered animals live their whole lives in these places. In Tar Heel, not far from my apartment in Wake Forest, 176,000 pigs are slaughtered each week. That's 9 million pigs annually.[13]

The high number of pigs being processed is really significant when you make the connection between these practices and their effects on the environment, people, our society, and the animals themselves. Bryan Walsh of *Time* magazine visited a factory farm and was able to skillfully describe its many effects:

A pig is being raised in a confined pen, packed in so tightly with other swine that their curly tails have been chopped off so they won't bite one another. To prevent him from getting sick in such close quarters, he is dosed with antibiotics. The waste produced by the pig and his thousands of pen mates on the factory farm where they live goes into manure lagoons that blanket neighboring communities with air pollution and a stomach-churning stench. He's fed on American corn. He's fed on American corn that was grown with the help of government subsidies and millions of tons of chemical fertilizer. When the pig is slaughtered, at about 5 months of age, he'll become sausage or bacon that will sell cheap, feeding an American addiction to meat that has contributed to an obesity epidemic currently afflicting more than two-thirds of the population. And when the rains come, the excess fertilizer that coaxed so much corn from the ground will be washed into the Mississippi River and down into the Gulf of Mexico, where it will help kill fish for miles and miles around. That's the state of your bacon—circa 2009.[14]

The practice of factory farming should bother us on many levels. We have already learned that God loves all creation, even the animals. He works to preserve it and wants all life to flourish. He has asked us to benevolently steward creation in a way that honors and glorifies Him. Treating living things as inanimate objects oversteps the bounds of stewardship. We have the right to use animals for food, but we don't have the right to act in cruel, cavalier ways toward God's creation or inflict unnecessary suffering on any living creature.

These practices run deeper than just animal rights. They deeply damage the environment and harm people. The 10 billion animals processed in America every year affect the quality of our air, rivers, and streams. According to the EPA, the agriculture and meat industries contribute to nearly three-quarters of all our water-quality problems. People are also affected. The fatty meat produced from these practices promotes obesity and affects global hunger issues. Over 800 million people in the world are hungry or malnourished. The majority of corn and soy our world produces now goes to feed cattle, pigs, and chickens.[15]

Americans can and should do better. The divine plan doesn't require vegetarianism or the abolition of meat, but factory farming is a destructive practice and our addiction to meat only complicates things. The apostle Paul said that everything we do—even our eating habits—should glorify God (1 Cor. 10:31). This means reforming our current system and implementing a healthier balance of foods, including more of the many wonderful fruits and vegetables God has given us, into our diets. Overconsumption of meat is not unlike our relentless pursuit of technology, toys, and money.

God's plan beckons us to become Christ-centered, people-loving consumers.

MUCH-NEEDED CHANGE

I often worry that one day, a hundred or more years from now, a student in a college religion class will do a project on American Christianity during my lifetime and wonder, *What blinded these people to God's plan? How could they have been so wrong?* I fear that one day, men and women will look back on us with the confusion that we now project onto mid-nineteenth-century Americans who turned a blind eye to slavery and racism.

Sidney Poitier is one of the most revered actors in American history. In 1963, he became the first black American to win an Academy Award for Best Actor. His films are often embroidered with social commentary, and his roles defied racial stereotypes. *Guess Who's Coming to Dinner* and *A Raisin in the Sun* are widely considered classics.

I stumbled across his book *Life Beyond Measure: Letters to My Great-Granddaughter.* Sidney is a wonderful writer. The book is an attempt to pass on the wisdom he amassed over decades to his great-granddaughter, Ayele. In one chapter, he addresses the state of our environment:

We're now at a place where we have begun to tabulate our obligations to the environment rather than the environment's obligations to us.... When we first came, the environment was ready to receive us, and it nurtured us. It was so massive, so pure, and so thunderously healthy that we had no need to worry for generations upon generations whether it would be able to sustain itself on our behalf. In its infinite beauty, it has done that, but now things are different.

We are 6.4 or 6.5 billion human beings on the planet. The water supply is shortening. The amount of topsoil to produce food is dwindling. The remaining clean, fresh, unpolluted air for breathing and for nurturing all living things is being poisoned by substances incompatible to its health.

Pollutants foul our air and water, damaging the food supply in the oceans and on land. They threaten the very ozone that protects the earth's atmosphere. In our joy for life and our voracious consumption of resources, we have carelessly reached a critical point in our own survival. Even yet, Ayele, as I sit here, many people are reluctant to accept the responsibility that rests with us all to pursue answers to the problems and, as we find them, to engage in them.

As a society, we have grown to prefer the easy over the difficult, the quick over the slow, the cheap over the costly—and those choices are not often to the benefit of nature.[16]

From Black Friday to bankruptcy, from factory farming to mountaintop removal mining, we have become comfortable with the collateral damage produced by our lives. Do we choose the easy, the quick, and the cheap even when God's plan requires the difficult, slow, and costly?

11

HOW GREEN IS
GREEN ENOUGH?

I didn't recognize the phone number flashing across my phone. It never crossed my mind that one of the greatest theologians alive was calling because he was struggling with creation care.

"Jonathan, I am a theologian. I can talk about God and the Bible and church history all day. I know what the Bible says about caring for creation. I know where the church has stood on this until recently," he said. "The problem I have—and the problem I think a lot of theologians are having—is the next step. We can talk about how much God loves the earth and wants us to care for it, but theologians aren't experts on living green. We don't know what to do next."

I bungled the conversation, pretended I was qualified to advise such a great mind. When I hung up the phone, I realized (and he probably did too) that I was struggling with the same question. The "What should we do next?" is plaguing more than just intellectuals. Environmental issues are complicated and involve morality, economics, politics, and science.

Environmentalists are often reluctant to speak about environmental trade-offs, but they come into play with almost every environmental decision. We need to begin developing renewable energy sources, yet, depending on where they construct the photovoltaic panels and wind turbines, the infrastructure and upkeep will have negative impacts on protected lands and endangered species.[1] We can stop using disposable diapers, but growing, harvesting, and producing cotton to make reusable diapers usually require extensive use of harmful chemicals. And cotton diapers require energy and water to wash, over and over again.[2] We need to decrease our dependence on foreign oil, but should we destroy God's creation to get it through offshore drilling and opening up wildlife reserves?

Newton's idea that every action has an opposing reaction holds true in the environmental realm. Every environmental solution involves trade-offs, either environmental or economic. These are complicated issues to evaluate, even for so-called experts, and this complexity has bred a terrible sense of competition among environmentalists. Everyone tries to prove why they are making all the right decisions and supporting the right policies and to show why others aren't.

Shortly after my own green conversion, I found it harrowing and, as an untrained person, experienced incredible amounts of guilt and frustration. I remember proudly sharing the news that I had finally switched all the bulbs in my house to compact fluorescents to save energy with someone who had been an environmentalist for some time.

"When you break one or one burns out, you recycle them, right?" she asked.

"Um . . . no. I throw them away."

She then proceeded to tell me that they contain traces of mercury, which poisons the earth and wildlife, so they must be recycled.

My face fell, and I felt chastened. "I guess I'm not green enough."[3]

Everyone who has consciously started trying to live a greener lifestyle has felt something similar to this. The neighbor who lives to the left of you doesn't recycle the way your family does, but the neighbor to the right composts. The accountant who lives in the cul-de-sac just bought a hybrid, but the telemarketer who lives on the corner rides his bike to work. Your best friend at work brings her own reusable canvas shopping bags to the grocery store, but the skinny guy in your church small group harvests food from his organic garden.

Who is greenest, and who is green enough? What lifestyle changes are most responsible, and how does one evaluate the viability of environmental policy and procedure? Who is abiding by the divine plan for our planet, and who is bulldozing his or her way to the hot place?

OUR MESSY FAITH

I am not going to provide a list of things you must do to be green. Plenty of good books serve as comprehensive guides for green living, and I list a few of them in the Recommended Resources appendix. This book is about God's heart and the state of our world. I do not have these issues completely figured out. I am on a journey. As a sojourner, I have not arrived at all the conclusions. God is still chiseling away.

Each policy and proposed solution must be evaluated on its own merits and in its own way. I don't have all the answers. I have included some good guidelines for living in sync with the divine plan in the Guidelines for a Greener Life appendix. These are only guidelines, not an exhaustive list.

The most important reason I won't provide a *Good Housekeeping*-style list of tips is because it would fill one of the most unholy longings inside us all: the hunger for rules. Man loves law. When everything is laid out, life is easy and clean. When we live under law, we always know what to do because it has been spelled out for us. That is why so many authors today claim to reduce the mystery and majesty of God to "Five Easy Steps to Purposeful Living" or "Seven Steps to Peace with God." This is a book of reflection on God's Word and God's world, God's written revelation and revelation through creation. I trust it will serve as a resource for you to make your own checklist.

God doesn't give us a checklist for solving every complex environmental issue. He doesn't tell us what car to drive or which household cleaners to purchase or if we should compost. He gives us principles, but every person applies those principles differently. Many people who love Jesus disagree on the most difficult environmental issues. Too much of Christian environmentalism has become law-driven, filled with litmus tests and dos and don'ts and guilt and judgmentalism.

> 🍇 God doesn't give us a checklist for solving every complex environmental issue.

If you carpool with a buddy to work, great. If you swear off bottled water and carry a reusable container instead, wonderful. If you feel led to begin setting aside Sunday as a true Sabbath so that you don't drive or shop, good for you. If you do your research before making purchases so you don't patronize companies that irresponsibly dump sewage into lakes, pump incalculable amounts of smog into the air, and destroy the infrastructures of local communities, you'll make me smile. Perhaps you do some or all of these things and more, but when it comes to *many* environmental decisions, leave room for the Holy Spirit to do His job in guiding you.

Sometimes Christianity is messy. Much of Christianity is lived in the realm of conscience. It isn't always clear-cut or easy. Christian ethics is filled with moral dilemmas; Christian living is filled with mystery; Christian theology has its share of chaos. But a healthy helping of messiness is powerfully positive because in mess and uncertainty, faith becomes strong. Messiness makes us feel weak, it forces us to relinquish control to God.

God doesn't leave us unequipped or unprepared to address the issues of our day. He has given us powerful principles and commands that serve as a guide for making environmental decisions. He has given us His plan for all creation, and as we discover that plan, God is able to change the world through our transformed hearts, minds, attitudes, and behavior. God has empowered us to live life, not as powerless wanderers, but as powerful conquerors (Rom. 8:37). Through His plan, we have been given the tools in Scripture to address hardships, famine, global poverty, disease, nakedness, and eternal life.

Many believe the greatest passage in Scripture for Christian ethics is the one about the Ten Commandments in Exodus. But Jesus actually gave us a principle that He said was the foundation for all the law and the prophets and is greater than any other commandment found anywhere in Scripture.

Jesus was approached by one of the greatest theologians of His day, an "expert in the law," who asked a tough question: "Which commandment is most important?" Jesus didn't have to think or blink: "Love the Lord your God with all your heart and with all your soul and with all your mind. This is the first and greatest commandment. And the second is like it: Love your neighbor as yourself" (Matt. 22:34–40; see also Mark 12:28–34). It is simple but profound. In one short statement, Jesus has given us a perfectly foundational principle by which to live all of life in the divine plan.

I call this *the power of third place*. In this abbreviated axiom, Jesus gives us the order for living: God first, others second, and ourselves (which Jesus barely even mentions) in a distant third.

God First

As Jesus said, "Seek *first* the kingdom of God" (Matt. 6:33 ESV; italics added). In other words, we arrange our lives so that God is always first and foremost. We place God so far above everything else and make Him such a high priority that we can declare, "There is nothing and no one but You, God. No one!"[4] We serve an awesome and jealous God whose desires must be placed high above all else. Our desire should be to love what God loves, to obey what God commands, to do what God asks, and to glorify Him to all people in every way possible. If we do anything less than this, our lives are an utter failure.

Creation isn't divine. Only God is divine. But Creation *is* sacred and therefore worthy of our respect. The great commandment to love God implies that we should treat what God has made with respect and care. If you love a parent, sibling, spouse, friend, or neighbor, you would certainly treat his or her belongings respectfully. The same should be offered to God.

Therefore, our actions must always consider God's commands about what He has made. Everything we do and even the policies we support must reflect the love God has for the creation He called "good." As Francis Schaeffer said, "If I love the Lover, I love what the Lover has made.… It is easy to make professions of faith, but they may not be worth much because they have little meaning. They may become merely a mental assent that means little or nothing."[5] Every Sunday in churches all across America, people are professing great love for God with their lips. We must also profess that sentiment every day with our lives.

Christianity is often lived in self-limitation. As the apostle Paul has said, some things that I am able to do I shouldn't do because they aren't God-glorifying (1 Cor. 10:23). I could justify a list of things, but many of them aren't wise or best. It is not the letter of the law but the spirit that gives life. To live within the divine plan for our planet, I must be relentlessly asking myself what will bring God the most glory.

Others Second

In Matthew 22 and Mark 12, Jesus added that the second greatest commandment was to love our neighbors. Jesus' call to consider our neighbor is perhaps no more relevant than in this discussion. The way I live affects people all over the world. It is absolutely impossible to separate the environment from our neighbors. The pollutants that we pump into our air show up in the breast milk of mothers in other continents and the blood of people living on the other side of the globe. The choice of lightbulbs we place in our homes has a profound effect on childhood asthma rates.[6] Neighbor-love must be the engine that drives my God-glorifying life.

"Others" include any alive today who depend on the earth's resources, not just those who live in our communities. Others also extend to those who are yet to be born. Edmund Burke famously noted that society is a contract between past and future generations as well as present generations. Each is critical in this process. The past generation provides the wisdom of experience to forge new solutions to today's problems, the present generation provides much-needed manpower to push the solutions forward, and future generations powerfully motivate us to keep fighting even when we begin to tire out.

When we place others first, we bring God glory. We cannot make the mistake of preserving the creation at the expense of humankind's well-being. It surely brings God glory to preserve a forest, but it also brings Him glory to find sustainable and creative ways to transform wood to make shelter. God has promised to supply all of our needs, and it brings Him glory when we allow His creation to provide for us. As Francis Schaeffer said, we are to "honor what God has made, up to the very highest level...without sacrificing man."[7]

God has promised to provide for our *needs*, which doesn't mean we are children in God's candy shop. The Bible teaches that when we ask in faith, God will answer our request. Philippians 4:19 says, "My God will meet all your needs according to His glorious riches in Jesus Christ." Yet James 4:3 elaborates on this idea: "When you ask, you do not receive, because you ask with wrong motives, that you may spend what you get on your pleasures."

Too many people today see God as a heavenly bellhop who is here to serve our every desire. They would never use that metaphor, but their actions tattle on them. God is infinitely above us, and He does not serve us. We exist to serve Him and serve others. It is wrongheaded to twist the Scriptures into prayers for God-given luxury cars and palatial homes. Rather than see God as the divine allowance-giver, we must recognize that God promises us only basic necessities. Any prosperity we experience should be used to first bring God glory and second to bless others.

You Third

This is the hardest part of the whole equation. When Jesus claims that we should love our neighbors as ourselves, He is not saying we should love ourselves and others equally. He implicitly accepts that we humans love ourselves and is telling us that we should turn that sentiment outward. Because Jesus barely mentions us in this passage, we conclude that concern for ourselves falls in a distant third.

Jesus actually teaches us to reject our self-love or me-first inclinations and to place ourselves last. It is "the Great Reversal" (Mark 10). Jesus asks us to be last, to place ourselves in the back of the line, to refuse the seat at the head of the table. In Matthew 20 and Luke 13, Jesus says that the last shall be first and the first shall be last. In Luke 9, Jesus asks us to "deny" ourselves.

It isn't as easy as it sounds. Ever since Adam and Eve snacked on forbidden fruit, we humans have been putting our desires first. Things haven't changed a lot since the Tower of Babel. We struggle with the same temptation they faced: that nothing that we want to do would be impossible for us (Gen. 11:6). We are tempted to assume the role of God, to place ourselves first, to step over the bounds of our humanity.

When I was a child in Sunday School, I learned a profound acronym that has stuck with me. J-O-Y: Jesus in first place, others in second place, and yourself in third place. I was unaware that this was such a powerful principle when I was learning it as a child. Now I am convinced it is the most practical, comprehensive, foolproof, easy-to-use principle for applying the divine plan to my life. Every habit I nurture, every dollar I spend, every corporation I patronize, every policy I support, the food I eat, the things I do for entertainment—every aspect of my life should be tested by this principle. I must constantly ask myself which practice, purchase, policy, meal, or habit places God and His revealed desires first, the well-being and care of others second, and my naturally

> 🍇 We are tempted to assume the role of God, to place ourselves first, to step over the bounds of our humanity.

selfish and greedy desires last. My corrupted propensity is to live this acrostic in reverse. I want to live with me in first place. Living life in this order, a Y-O-J life, is called *sin*.

In environmental discussions, we often talk about economics before we talk about compassion. We place ourselves and our wallets in first place. In second place, we often put others—at least the ones who benefit us in some way. Finally, we throw God the scraps. Some Christians working in Washington, DC, are promoting Y-O-J policies and calling them "Christian." Every Christian—especially those in the public sector—must be careful not to invert God's priorities, not to sell his or her biblical theology for a political ideology. Too often policy makers want to know what will make our bank accounts increase rather than promote things that magnify God. When we accept this sort of thinking, we replace need with greed, and like Esau, sell our birthright for a worthless bowl of pottage.

Promoting a Y-O-J lifestyle violates Scripture by placing humans at the center of creation and gives Christians a terrible reputation. Christians are to be beacons for compassion, conservation, generosity, and sustainability in the public square. If we who bear the name of Christ, from the White House to my house, reevaluate our lives in light of the teachings of God's Word and the conditions of God's world, nonbelievers would be more receptive to the Christian message.

Often conservative Christians devalue nature by placing man at the center of the universe. Often secular environmentalists overvalue nature by devaluing man. The divine plan presents a third way: valuing God above all else, loving others, and bestowing on creation the honor and respect that God has given it.

We are most powerful when we reject the urge to elevate humanity and instead seek to glorify God and promote the well-being of others. We expose the power to solve problems, create community, and promote life and health when we place God first and ourselves last. When our lives are guided by the Grand Reversal and the greatest commandments, the gospel of Jesus Christ will penetrate into hearts and minds.

I don't know anything that's more powerful—and green—than that.

12

SOMETHING'S RUMBLING

SEVERAL months after my epiphany-inspired creation care initiative had created an unexpected media firestorm, I decided to meet with two of my mentors at Bahama Breeze Restaurant, just off the interstate. We reminisced about my television and radio appearances, my interviews in magazines and newspapers, and my opportunities to speak across the country. I was feeling pretty puffed up as my two friends took turns patting me on the back.

"Did you see the write-up in the *Dallas Morning News*?" one friend asked as he laid another news story in front of me. The headline read, "Younger Evangelicals Are Taking Movement in a New Direction."

I was no longer interested in the coconut shrimp.

The column recounted my initiative and how it tied into a national trend of evangelicalism's broadening agenda. With each word I swelled with pride. How did I miss this juicy story? "Whenever a 25-year-old can get the attention of the Southern Baptist Convention, you know something's rumbling," the last sentence said.[1] My eyes twinkled, and I considered reading it aloud for the benefit of the restaurant's other patrons. *I have really done something*, I thought. *I have made quite a name for myself.* I motioned for the waiter to bring an extra chair to hold my ego as I looked back down at the article to admire my work.

I continued to read, and then my eyes widened at something dreadful: the article's conclusion was not about me. The article addressed something greater. The great line in the climactic conclusion didn't even call me by name. It referred to a nameless "25-year-old." Like a pin to my prideful balloon, my moment in the sun became heatstroke.

I realized that scouring the Scriptures in search of God's plan and working on Christian environmental initiatives placed me in community with many wonderful people and organizations that have long been blazing the creation care trail. When the writer for the *Dallas Morning News* shared his amazement that a twenty-five-year-old could capture the attention of such a large audience, he was applauding my entire generation. What surprises him is not me, but hundreds of thousands like me who are mobilizing neighborhood clean-up days, writing letters to congressmen, volunteering in community improvement organizations, petitioning pastors for more outwardly focused programming, and promoting the Scripture's teachings on these issues. As followers of Jesus are discovering the divine plan, they aren't able to sit still and do nothing. They are compelled to act and lead others to follow.

Followers of Jesus are striving to live healthier, sustainable lives. People are increasingly reforming their churches, turning the tide of concern in favor of a more compassionate, holistic Christianity.

Tim Wolfe is a good friend and the founding pastor of

1027 Church in downtown Atlanta. 1027 meets in a progressive, artsy neighborhood and seeks to disciple Christians who don't just gather weekly but also live daily as the hands and feet of Jesus Christ in culture. Sensing the need to be more intentional in caring for creation, Tim began serving fair-trade coffee in reusable ceramic mugs on Sunday mornings. Rather than have the "paper, plastic, or Styrofoam" debate, he decided to go all the way.

It sounds insignificant. How much difference can reusable mugs and fair-trade coffee really make on the environment? I believe this church's effort will have an immeasurable effect. The money from the coffee goes to post-genocide Rwandan farmers through a ministry called Land of a Thousand Hills. This company is giving hope to thousands of Africans every day. By switching to ceramic mugs, this congregation's Sunday coffee service now produces almost no waste.

Less notably but of equal importance is the way this affects the church culture. Sustainable living has become a natural outflow of Christ-followship for 1027 members. Families will begin to think twice in their own homes. They may opt for mugs at their own parties and birthday celebrations, even when plastic cups would be easier. Children who grow up in the 1027 culture will see sustainability as normative. When they have families and attend other churches, they will promote the same ideals in those churches. As with a pebble in a big pond, the ripples are enormous. When a guest comes to 1027, he or she is handed a mug as a way of saying, "This is what we do. Come be a part of this." Every Sunday, the church people gather to sip on steaming coffee and share their lives with each other. With regard to the divine plan, it is church at its finest.

At Cross Pointe, the church where I serve and teach, we've also begun making changes. We've started recycling the weekly waste in the offices and switching to energy-efficient lighting. In turn, we've saved money on our utility costs. Our Sunday worship guides are now printed on recycled paper with soy-based ink. The message on the back of the worship guide says, "Because of our obedience to God's Word (Genesis 2:15) and our love for people who depend on our planet's resources, this worship guide has been printed on recycled paper." We just opened a one-mile long nature trail where families can connect with creation.

Stories like these are emerging everywhere. While we still need to improve, the divine plan is certainly taking hold in many places. God is on the move. God's people are on the move.

The many wonderful stories I hear and people I meet give me a reason to smile and hope for a better tomorrow. Yet some are still skeptical. Among environmentalists, and even Christian environmental advocates, many believe that humanity has passed the point of no return. They think things are too bad, people are too clueless, and habits are too destructive and ingrained for things to turn around. This mind-set is displayed in depressing films like Leonardo DiCaprio's documentary *The 11th Hour* and the History Channel's *Life After People*, which features images of Manhattan reminiscent of *I Am Legend*. If they *really* believe this to be true, I wonder why they devote their lives to "hopeless" causes.

Those who believe our world is doomed and beyond help don't recognize the very first principle we learn in Genesis: God has power over the planet. We serve a God who wants this creation to flourish, and He is capable of restoring even the most run-down corner of Earth. Rather than ask whether or not the world is beyond help, we need to persist in restoring it and trust God to do what He does well—bring healing.

We take environmental action, not because we are guaranteed success, but because we know success is only reached through pressing on. I believe the naysayers are wrong. I believe that our problems, while dire, are not beyond the reach of our caring Creator. He wants to work healing miracles in our world, and He wants to use us to do it.

The environment will be beyond help, be truly dilapidated when we quit working together to search out problems and, as we find them, attempt to solve them. When we stop using our God-given means to accomplish our God-given task of stewarding this world, our world will truly be in disrepair. Earth will be beyond our care when give-up-itis sets in, when discouragement becomes defeatism, when we forget that we do not fight this battle alone but alongside an all-powerful God who presides over the destiny of this planet.

New voices are ascending into positions of leadership and influence, and they can translate the divine plan into progress, hope, and change. Something is rumbling among Christ followers. I am encouraged that an increasing number of Christians are bringing healing to God's creation via their homes, churches, and communities.

Many in rising generations feel like those of the Kennedy generation in the 1960s, whom JFK spoke to in his inaugural address: "I do not believe that any of us would exchange places with any other people or any other generation. The energy, the faith, the devotion which we bring to this endeavor will light our country and all who serve it—and the glow from that fire can truly light the world."

Transformation, redemption, compassion, and creation care are not options for us; they are our calling. Along with creation care are poverty and justice, hunger and war. Hurting orphans and hungry grandmothers wait for us to raise our voices. God's Word demands that we minister in culture, politics, and media. Everyday we wake up and are faced with a choice to do nothing or make a difference. We either follow our own plans for life or pursue the divine plan for our planet. We either ignore the desire of God's heart for our world or embrace it. Let's clinch the task God has given us and transform this place called Earth into a garden where the creation will sing hymns about the Creator and the gospel of Jesus Christ will flourish.

GUIDELINES FOR A GREENER LIFE

There is no instruction manual in Scripture that lays out what we must do to earn a "good steward" trophy. The Bible does, however, contain a litany of creation care principles, which should inform the way we live.

Guided by those principles, I have compiled a list of best practices, which may be helpful to you. Many of these come from my own life and can serve as a guide for your household. My suggestion is to implement one change per week or one per month, adding more as time goes on.

Energy Reduction

- *Turn off the juice:* When I was growing up, my parents would always say, "When not in use, turn off the juice." This meant "Turn off the light and quit wasting energy, stupid." Take their advice and turn off the lights when you leave a room. Also unplug any electronic appliances that are not in use because they will still use energy even though they aren't technically functioning.

• *Less energy, more money*: Replace your incandescent lightbulbs with compact fluorescent ones. It will save you money and use less than half the energy. Also make sure that your house has appropriate amounts of insulation for the climate where you live, and when the money is available, update your home with energy-efficient windows and ceiling fans. If your HOA allows it, line-dry your clothes and avoid the dryer. In addition to reducing the emissions given off to make the superfluous energy, you will be surprised how much money you will save on utilities by adopting these practices.

Simpler Living

• *Old school*: It is hard to improve on something that is already great, and many of the staple green items of old have been improved. I use a reel mower, for example, which cuts my grass perfectly and doesn't use any gas, and I always use reusable glasses and mugs over disposable ones. You could also plant a garden where you grow your own fruits, herbs, and vegetables and learn to make many of the items that you currently purchase.

• *Keep it local*: Whenever you are able to buy from a local farmer, artist, or tradesman, do it. It will cut out the middleman, give money to a person rather than a corporation, and radically cut down on the environmental impact of the good purchased.

• *R & R*: When you are looking to relax, try leaving the television and computer off. Play a board game, go outside, chat with a neighbor, or curl up and read a good book. Good old-fashioned fun is wonderful.

Consumption

• *Recycle:* This is the most basic thing anyone can do to steward the earth. It makes sense, it's easy, and no one has ever been able to give me a reason for not doing it. In short, if you don't recycle, you should be ashamed of yourself. Also, make sure that the goods you purchase are stored in recyclable containers. If you throw a lot of food out as organic waste, consider composting.

• *Buy smarter:* Used items are best because no new materials are spent, and local goods are second best. Other than those, take the time to find out where things are made and where your money is going before you make a purchase. If you are buying paper products, look for the one made from postconsumer recycled content. Also, don't skimp on a cheaply made item that will break in a year or two. Invest in quality goods that will last as long as possible. If you are purchasing appliances or electronics, make sure the item is Energy Star rated.

• *No bags:* Using disposable plastic shopping bags is difficult to justify. Always carry reusable canvas bags in your car. If you forget them, carry your items by hand and be grateful that you can do ten minutes less on the elliptical.

• *Food for thought:* Again, local is best whether you are buying food or eating out. At the grocery store, remember that organic is better for you and the earth than overprocessed goods. Also, cut down on your meat intake to reduce your environmental impact. If you are a coffee drinker, make sure you purchase only fair-trade coffee.

• *Water you doing:* Purchasing bottled water is rarely necessary. Bottled water is a good that proves time and time again to be no better or tastier than the alternative. Purchase a good reusable bottle and make it your new best friend. If you use water on your lawn or in your garden, purchase a rain barrel. If you are in the market for a washing machine, go with a water-saving front loader. Low-flow toilets are also ideal, and you should always be careful that the chemicals you are putting down your drain or in the soil aren't environmentally destructive.

Transportation

- *Double up:* If you are able to carpool anywhere, do it. With high gas prices, there is never a better time to start. Also, give public transportation a try if it is available. It isn't as intimidating as you think.

- *Go zero:* I'm lazy, but I am trying to learn that if it is feasible to walk somewhere, I probably should. A bike is also a great investment that has the added benefit of working off that spare tire.

- *Car smarts:* Though some exceptions to this rule exist, smaller is always better and a minivan is preferable to an SUV. Hybrids are great, but pricey. Go with the most fuel-efficient model available. Avoid fast acceleration in town and high speeds on the highway, and make sure your tires have adequate air pressure.

Advocacy

- *Use your voice:* As Americans, we have the privilege of being involved in the political process. Get informed on environmental issues through nonpartisan sources and then vote accordingly. If a creation care issue is up for a vote by your representative, write or call your congressman. Just get involved.

• *Mobilize:* Make sure to influence your peers. Tell them how much money you are saving and share with them all the reasons you have chosen to live differently. Share the divine plan with them. Organize a rally or begin a social change project in your community. Perhaps you'll choose to pick up litter in your local park or clean up a neighborhood pond. It doesn't matter. Just get people moving!

THE BIG, BAD CLIMATE QUESTION

No environmental issue causes blood pressures to rise, lips to quiver, fists to ball, and brows to furrow like global warming, or its more accurate and less abrasive moniker *climate change*. Just mention this issue in a room of mixed political and intellectual company and you will witness senior citizens coming to blows and family ties cracking right before your eyes. Seriously. New historical evidence indicates that the reason the Hatfields had a beef with the McCoys was because the McCoys believed in climate change. Okay. Not really. But the fervor surrounding this issue is reaching fever pitch.

Let me tell you how explosive and divisive this issue is. Not long ago, I was interviewed by a regional newspaper on creation care. At one point, the journalist interviewing me asked a direct question about climate change, and I took what is undoubtedly a middle-of-the-road position. The article came out, and I didn't think anymore about it. Unfortunately, others did. In the twenty-four hours following the article's publication, I received more than 200 e-mails ranging from tear-driven applause to implied death threats. Really.

The debate surrounding this issue is crying out for a rational, distinctly Christian position. Rather than tell each other what to believe or belittle each other for disagreeing, it seems more profitable for us to adopt a commonsense, principled, disarming approach to this explosive issue. I call this the Virtue-Driven Method:

Honesty

Any time we begin discussing an issue, it is best to begin with the facts. We must always be honest about the facts regarding any issue, even when we don't like them or they don't support our stance. The facts on this issue are simple: we have more than a century's worth of temperature records, and the analysis of all these records show a rise in global average surface air temperature. This doesn't mean that there have not been cooler years or winters with record lows along the way, but the trend has been steadily upward.

That trend by itself would be worrisome enough and would cause us to consider what measures we should take to adapt to a changing climate. But another trend accompanies this one: the proportion of carbon dioxide in the atmosphere has nearly doubled from its background level, mostly because of human action. This second trend is inarguable, and the link between burning fossil fuels and deforestation and the rising level of carbon dioxide in the atmosphere is ironclad.

More than a century ago in the mid-1890s, scientists began pondering the connection between those two observable trends: what would happen to all the carbon dioxide added to the atmosphere from human activities in the industrial era? Then in the 1930s, when the warming trend was large enough to be detectable, scientists began to argue about a possible connection between carbon dioxide and temperature. After World War II, meteorological data from around the globe were gathered on a much larger scale, and in the 1960s and 1970s, computers were first used to crunch those numbers.[1]

In more recent years, weather satellites vastly expanded our ability to measure what is happening on the surface of the earth, even in places where weather stations are absent. Direct and indirect historical evidence about temperature and carbon dioxide has been assembled from historical records, tree rings, pollen in lake sediments, and air trapped in deep layers of snow from many years ago. There's still a lot that scientists don't know, but the base of information is much broader than it used to be. Those are the facts.

We must also be honest that today a large majority of scientists engaged in this issue think that it is very likely that humans are contributing to much, if not most, of the warming we are seeing. This position has been endorsed by the National Academies of Science for virtually every developed country, including the United States, Japan, Russia, the United Kingdom, France, and China.[2] In the U.S. alone, the evidence has garnered support from NASA's Goddard Institute, National Oceanic and Atmospheric Administration, Environmental Protection Agency, American Geophysical Union, American Institute of Physics, National Center for Atmospheric Research, and American Meteorological Society. These organizations and institutes have produced countless papers and statements on the subject.

Acknowledging the majority opinion does not necessarily mean these scientists are right in their conclusions—after all, all human enterprises are fraught with pride, bias, ignorance, and uncertainty. But scientists themselves (honest scientists, that is) don't claim to be absolutely certain. They just claim to be a lot surer about the connection between greenhouse gas pollution and warming than when they first started comprehensively assessing the research in the 1980s. Honesty compels us to admit that the general agreement connecting human action to a changing climate includes most climate scientists.

On the other hand, we must be honest that consensus doesn't mean unanimity. Some sincere, respected climate scientists offer alternative causes and/or solutions for climate change. We must recognize that these individuals are not "quacks," and their reasons for holding to their positions should be examined. It is possible that the sincere minority is right, and the majority wrong. We have to be honest about that, too.

Integrity

I recently debated a Christian environmentalist at a nearby university. In the first twenty minutes, he claimed to be an expert scientist, economist, ethicist, theologian, and policy analyst. I could hardly believe it, but he is like a lot of people today.

As Christians, we should have enough integrity never to pretend we are experts on something when we are not. We must first maintain occupational integrity. Too many Americans pretend that they have received special training as scientists that allows them to assess the validity of climate science properly. I've received many e-mails from opinionated folks saying, "I have extensively researched this issue," by which they mean "I've read a lot of blogs." Let's be clear: neither frequent viewership of Fox News nor owning a copy of *An Inconvenient Truth* makes one "an expert." Furthermore, we must have the theological integrity not to twist Scripture in such a way as to pretend it offers special revelation about whether global warming is occurring and, if it is occurring, whether people are causing it.

Scriptures seem to affirm that God created a planet that has inherent stability, and that stability helps human civilization flourish, just as the human body has a stability that helps ward off infections and heal from injuries. But neither human bodies nor the climate system appears to be infinitely stable. We know that it is possible to do damage, both intentionally and unintentionally.

In the spirit of integrity, we must do our best to ignore the extreme positions and evaluate this important issue with a level head. That means ignoring positions like the one espoused by ABC newsman Bill Blakemore who said, "Climate isn't the story of our time; it's the only story,"[3] as well as those people who emotionally deny present realities without proper education.

Integrity also means that we should avoid the apocalyptic claims that our actions will lead to the destruction of the planet. If climate scientists are right, ignoring climate change will cause a lot of people unnecessary suffering and will shorten many lives. But it won't cause the extinction of the human race, as some seem to claim. This world will end when God decides it will and not a second or season before. Having integrity means ignoring the claims of those who say that action on climate change is an evil subterfuge to undermine the economy, destroy capitalism, or institute socialism. Climate policy will have big effects on the economy, not all of them benign, and those are worthy of debate. Yet we shouldn't impugn the motives of those who honestly believe that the magnitude of the problem requires big actions.

Justice

I think we have to admit that, if the majority view of climate scientists is right, poor people will suffer more from floods, droughts, disease, water shortage, and crop failure than rich people—like you and me—will. But the same asymmetry afflicts current policies proposed to solve the problem of climate change: a rise in the price of energy will affect poor people more than rich people. The poor always suffer from disruption, whether from climate change or policy change.

As Christians, compassion compels us to offer hope and help to those in need. Both climate change believers and skeptics can agree that we must be willing to build the right bridges, offer international assistance, and direct aid from both private philanthropy and government to help poor people withstand disasters like floods, storms, and drought, whether or not they are caused by human-induced global warming. We can't get so swept up into climate politics that we fail to work on behalf of the poor and vulnerable. Christians should always be guided by a sense of compassion and justice.

Prudence

Whenever we discuss issues that affect human lives and the balanced order of the natural world, we must keep prudence in our hearts. Even in the absence of perfect knowledge or unanimity, we have to make informed decisions about positions and policy. This means taking a position of prudence based partly on science that is inevitably changing. We can, and often do, make wise decisions in the absence of infallible evidence.

These virtues, when applied, seem to indicate that though the claims of science are neither infallible nor unanimous, they are substantial and cannot be dismissed out of hand on either scientific or theological grounds. There is not enough evidence to dismiss the high likelihood that the earth's climate is warming as a partial result of human actions, and the people at highest risk are the poorest on earth. Moreover, the pollution we emit each year stays in the atmosphere and contributes to warming for decades or even centuries, and our pollution is accelerating rather than leveling off. If the consensus view is right, then we're digging a deeper and deeper hole. Therefore, it seems to follow that we Christians should be proactive in taking responsibility for our contributions to climate change—however great or small—and engage the issue through wise solutions. In the face of conflicting evidence, Christians should always act prudently. If we do this, we will maintain clean hands before a cynical world and pure hearts before a holy God no matter what science concludes in the years to come.

RESOURCES

By listing these resources, I am not endorsing them in their entirety. I am merely listing the broad range of websites and books that I used in my study of this subject. I encourage my readers to check out these resources and others in a spirit of openness and discernment.

Helpful Websites

www.flourishonline.org: Home of *Flourish* magazine, the nation's premier creation care periodical.

www.sustainlane.com: Great resource for environmental news and tips, with a whole section devoted to faith-based creation care.

www.Farmersmarket.com: A directory of farmers' markets all across the United States.

www.energystar.gov: A great resource on energy-efficient products and practices for your home and business.

www.epa.gov/greenvehicles: The EPA has a great rating system for cars available on its Web site.

www.erideshare.com: A free place to meet people in your area who are interested in carpooling.

www.gogreentube.com: A green version of YouTube that is filled with helpful videos that educate, inspire, and teach environmentally friendly practices.

www.fueleconomy.gov: Find fuel economy information on traditional, hybrid, and alternative-fuel vehicles.

www.41pounds.org: A nonprofit organization working to eliminate the massive amounts of junk mail Americans receive. Register your address and stop the mailbox madness. (Also see http://mailstopper.tonic.com/.)

www.earth911.org: A website offering recycling centers for every good imaginable. Look up the item in its database, and a location near you is provided.

www.worldofgood.com: A website offering direct-from-the-source goods that support a charitable cause or are people-positive, eco-positive, or animal-friendly.

www.myfootprint.org/en: Wonder what your ecological footprint looks like? This website will calculate it for you.

www.pesticideinfo.org: A searchable and comprehensive list of toxic chemicals and nontoxic alternative solutions.

www.foodnews.org: Check out the "Shopper's Guide to Pesticides in Produce." It is a great tool for grocery store planning.

Books

Abbate, Michael. *Gardening Eden: How Creation Care Will Change Your Faith, Your Life, and Our World.* Colorado Springs, CO: Waterbrook Press, 2009.

Achtemeier, Elizabeth. *Nature, God and Pulpit.* Grand Rapids, MI: Wm. B. Eerdmans Publishing Company, 1992.

Barnes-Davies, Rebecca. *50 Ways to Save the Earth: How You and Your Church Can Make a Difference.* Louisville, KY: Westminster John Knox Press, 2009.

Bouma-Prediger, Steven. *For the Beauty of the Earth: A Christian Vision for Creation Care*. Grand Rapids, MI: Baker Academic, 2001.

Brown, Edward R. *Our Father's World: Mobilizing the Church to Care for Creation*. Downers Grove, IL: Intervarsity Press, 2008.

Campolo, Tony. *How to Rescue the Earth without Worshipping Nature: A Christian's Call to Save Creation*. Nashville, TN: Thomas Nelson Publishers, 1992.

DeWitt, Calvin B. *Earth-Wise: A Biblical Response to Environmental Issues*. 2nd ed. Grand Rapids, MI: Faith Alive Christian Resources, 2007.

Emanuel, Kerry. *What We Know About Climate Change*. Cambridge, MA: MIT Press, 2007.

Fowler, Robert Booth. *The Greening of Protestant Thought*. Chapel Hill, NC: University of North Carolina Press, 1995.

Friedman, Thomas L. *Hot, Flat, and Crowded: Why We Need a Green Revolution—And How It Can Renew America*. New York: Farrar, Straus and Giroux, 2008.

Frost, Michael. *Exiles: Living Missionally in a Post-Christian Culture*. Peabody, MA: Hendrickson Publishers, 2006.

Gingrich, Newt, and Terry L. Maple. *A Contract with the Earth*. Baltimore: Johns Hopkins University Press, 2007.

Gottlieb, Roger S. *A Greener Faith: Religious Environmentalism and Our Planet's Future*. Oxford: Oxford University Press, 2006.

Henson, Robert. *The Rough Guide to Climate Change: The Symptoms, the Science, the Solutions*. New York: Rough Guides Ltd., 2006.

Jenkins, Willis J. *Ecologies of Grace: Environmental Ethics and Christian Theology*. Oxford: Oxford University Press, 2008.

Kolbert, Elizabeth. *Field Notes from a Catastrophe: Man, Nature, and Climate Change.* New York: Bloomsbury Publishing, 2006.

Kostigen, Thomas, and Elizabeth Rogers. *The Green Book: The Everyday Guide to Saving the Planet One Simple Step at a Time.* New York: Three Rivers Press, 2007.

Land, Richard, and Louis Moore. *The Earth Is the Lord's: Christians and the Environment.* Nashville, TN: Baptist Sunday School Board, 1992.

LeQuire, Stan L., ed. *The Best Preaching on Earth: Sermons on Caring for Creation.* Valley Forge, PA: Judson Press, 1996.

Lomborg, Bjorn. *The Skeptical Environmentalist: Measuring the Real State of the World.* Cambridge: Cambridge University Press, 1998.

Louv, Richard. *Last Child in the Woods: Saving Our Children from Nature-Deficit Disorder.* Chapel Hill, NC: Algonquin Books, 2008.

Lowe, Ben. *Green Revolution: Coming Together to Care for Creation.* Downers Grove, IL: Intervarsity Press, 2009.

McGrath, Alister. *The Open Secret: A New Vision for Natural Theology.* Hoboken, NJ: Wiley-Blackwell, 2008.

——. *The Reenchantment of Nature: The Denial of Religion and the Ecological Crisis.* New York: Doubleday & Co., 2002.

McKnight, Scott. *The Jesus Creed: Loving God, Loving Others.* Brewster, MA: Paraclete Press, 2005.

Monsma, Steve. *Healing for a Broken World: Christian Perspectives on Public Policy.* Wheaton, IL: Crossway Books, 2008.

Northcott, Michael. *The Environment and Christian Ethics.* Cambridge: Cambridge University Press, 1996.

Oelschlaeger, Max. *Caring for Creation: An Ecumenical Approach to Environmental Ethics.* New Haven, CT: Yale University Press, 1994.

Pearce, Fred. *Confessions of an Eco-Sinner: Tracking Down the Sources of My Stuff*. Boston: Beacon Press, 2008.

Robinson, Tri with Jason Chatraw. *Saving God's Green Earth: Rediscovering the Church's Responsibility to Environmental Stewardship*. Norcross, GA: Ampelon Publishing, 2006.

Samson, Will. *Enough: Contentment in an Age of Excess*. Colorado Springs, CO: David C. Cook, 2009.

Sarna, Nahum, ed. *The JPS Torah Commentary: Genesis*. Philadelphia: Jewish Publication Society, 1989.

Schaeffer, Francis A. *Pollution and the Death of Man*. Wheaton, IL: Crossway Books, 1970.

Schor, Juliet B. *The Overspent American: Why We Want What We Don't Need*. New York: HarperPerennial, 1998.

Scully, Matthew. *Dominion: The Power of Man, the Suffering of Animals, and the Call to Mercy*. New York: St. Martin's Griffin, 2002.

Sider, Ronald J. *Rich Christians in an Age of Hunger: Moving from Affluence to Generosity*. 5th ed. Nashville, TN: W Publishing Group, 1997.

Sleeth, Emma. *It's Easy Being Green: One Student's Guide to Serving God and Saving the Planet*. Grand Rapids, MI: Zondervan, 2008.

Sleeth, Matthew. *Serve God, Save the Planet: A Christian Call to Action*. Grand Rapids, MI: Zondervan, 2007.

Sleeth, Nancy. *Go Green, Save Green: A Simple Guide to Saving Time, Money, and God's Green Earth*. Carol Stream, IL: Tyndale House Publishers, 2009.

Steffen, Alex, ed. *Worldchanging: A User's Guide for the 21st Century*. New York: Abrams, 2008.

Stott, John. *Issues Facing Christians Today*. 4th ed. Grand Rapids, MI: Zondervan, 2006.

Waltke, Bruce K. *Genesis: A Commentary.* Grand Rapids, MI: Zondervan, 2001.

Walton, John H. *The NIV Application Commentary: Genesis.* Grand Rapids, MI: Zondervan, 2001.

Wann, David. *Simple Prosperity: Finding Real Wealth in a Sustainable Lifestyle.* New York: St. Martin's Griffin, 2007.

Wilson, E. O. *The Creation: An Appeal to Save Life on Earth.* New York: W. W. Norton and Company, 2006.

Wilson, Ken. *Jesus Brand Spirituality: He Wants His Religion Back.* Nashville, TN: Thomas Nelson Publishers, 2008.

Wise, Stephen M. *An American Trilogy: Death, Slavery, and Dominion on the Banks of the Cape Fear River.* Philadelphia: Da Capo Press, 2009.

Wright, Christopher J. H. *The Mission of God: Unlocking the Bible's Grand Narrative.* Downers Grove, IL: InterVarsity Press, 2006.

Wright, N. T. *Surprised by Hope: Rethinking Heaven, the Resurrection and the Mission of the Church.* New York: HarperOne, 2008.

Creation Care Organizations

A Rocha (www.arocha.org): An international organization that focuses on habitat conservation, biodiversity loss, and creation care education. A Rocha is one of the oldest and largest creation care organizations in existence.

Advent Conspiracy (www.adventconspiracy.org): A movement that seeks to inspire Christians to "worship fully, spend less, give more, and love all" by celebrating Christmas in a less consumerist way. Check out its site and consider having a more Christ-centered advent this year.

Au Sable Institute of Environmental Studies (www.ausable.org): A well-established organization seeking to promote Christian environmental stewardship through academic and community programming. Au Sable is especially famous for its college- and university-level creation care courses.

Blessed Earth (www.blessedearth.org): The nonprofit organization founded by Dr. Matthew and Nancy Sleeth that works with churches, campuses, and media to "build bridges that promote measurable environmental change and meaningful spiritual growth."

Care of Creation (www.careofcreation.org): An organization that combines missionary fervor with environmental stewardship. This organization works most intensely in Kenya and the United States.

Christians for the Mountains (www.Christiansforthemountains .org): A Christian network advocating for sustainable living and the responsible stewardship of the Appalachian Mountains. Its primary issue of concern is mountaintop-removal coal mining.

Creation, I Care (www.creationicare.org): The creation care ministry of Northland Church with Pastor Joel Hunter. This is a great model for local churches looking to begin a stewardship ministry.

Creation Care Study Program (www.creationcsp.org): An organization offering an "academic semester abroad connecting Christian faith with the most complex, urgent global issues of the coming decades." During the fall and spring semesters, CCSP offers programs in both Belize and the South Pacific.

Ecological Concerns for Hunger Organization (www.echonet.org): An inter-denominational Christian organization with a presence in 180 countries "to help those working internationally with the poor be more effective, especially in the area of agriculture."

Evangelical Environmental Network (www.creationcare.org): The founding organization of the Evangelical Climate Initiative, which works to influence public policy and shape local churches on issues such as climate change.

Floresta (www.floresta.org): An organization working to reverse deforestation and poverty through community development, innovative forestry, micro-enterprise, and Christian discipleship.

Flourish (www.flourishonline.org): A distinctly evangelical organization seeking to inspire and equip churches to better love God through sustainable living. Flourish offers a national Christian conference on creation care featuring some of America's most sought-after authors and thinkers. Also, check out *Flourish* magazine.

National Association of Evangelicals (http://www.nae.net): The NAE is a conglomerate of Evangelical denominations exerting a powerful voice on issues such as human rights, the sanctity of life, peace, justice, and creation care.

Plant with Purpose (www.plantwithpurpose.org): A Christian humanitarian organization working to break the cycle of poverty and deforestation by planting trees and offering Christian counseling and guidance.

Renewal (www.renewingcreation.org): A student-led creation care movement active on campuses throughout the United States and Canada. If you are a college student, check out Renewal and consider connecting students on your campus with this organization.

Restoring Eden (www.restoringeden.org): A Christian grassroots network dedicated to "encouraging faithful stewardship of the natural world as a biblical, moral, and wise value." Its primary areas of work are nature appreciation, environmental stewardship, and public advocacy.

Southern Baptist Environment and Climate Initiative (www.baptistcreationcare.org): An independent network of Southern Baptist pastors, leaders, and laypersons who believe in stewardship that is both biblically rooted and intellectually informed. Read the declaration and sign online.

NOTES

Introduction

1. Max Oelschlaegar, *Caring for Creation: An Ecumenical Approach to the Environmental Crisis* (New Haven, CT: Yale University Press, 1994), 5.

2. Holly Vicente Robaina, "It's Not Easy Being Green: How's a Christian to Respond to the Hot Button Issue of the Environment?" *Christianity Today*, March/April 2008, 54.

Chapter 1. My Green Awakening

1. LifeWay Research, "Protestant Pastors Split on Reality of Global Warming," May 2009, lifeway.com/common/clickthru/. . .?X=/file/?id=6964.

2. Guth, James L., et al., "Faith and the Environment: Religious Beliefs and Attitudes on Environmental Policy," *American Journal of Political Science* 39, May 1995, 1.

3. Robert Booth Fowler, *The Greening of Protestant Thought* (Chapel Hill, NC: University of North Carolina Press, 1995), 45.

4. Audrey Barrick, "Study: American, Christian Lifestyles Not Much Different," *Christian Post*, February 6, 2007, http://www.christianpost.com/article/20070206/25642_Study:_Americans

_Tune_More_Into_Indulgence;_Christians_No_Different
.htm.

5. Glenn Scherer, "Christian-Right Views Are Swaying Politicians and Threatening the Environment," *Grist Magazine*, October 27, 2004, http://www.grist.org/news/maindish/2004/10/27/ scherer-christian/.

Chapter 2. A Deeper Shade of Green

1. Mimi Spencer, "Is Green the New Black?" *Observer*, April 15, 2007, www.guardian.co.uk/lifeandstyle/2007/apr/15/fashion .features1/print.

2. Ibid.

3. Organic Trade Association, 2006 Manufacturer Survey, http:// www.ota.com/pics/documents/short%20overview%20MMS .pdf.

4. Marcelle Hopkins, "Green Is the New Black: Eco-Fashion Goes Mainstream," November 28, 2006, http://jscms.jrn.columbia .edu/cns/2006-11-28/hopkins-ecofashion. (Also try http://www .azcentral.com/ent/pop/articles/1129ecofashion1129.html)

5. Brian Wingfield, "Green: The New Black," *Forbes*, September 26, 2007.

6. Adam Lashinsky, "Be Green—Everybody's Doing It," *CNN Money.com*, July 12, 2006, http://money.cnn.com/ 2006/07/12/news/economy/pluggedin_lashinsky.fortune/ index.htm?section=money_topstories

7. Anonymous, "Vanity Fair Hails Green 'the New Black' on Eco-Unfriendly Paper: Will Environmentalism Wear Well as the Latest Fashion?" April 24, 2006, http://abcnews.go.com/ Entertainment/story?id=1883369&page=1.

8. For more on the unhealthy nature of both cultural responses, read the work of Mark Driscoll in *Radical Reformission* (Grand Rapids, MI: Zondervan, 2004).

9. Charles Colson and Ellen Santilli Vaughn, *The Body* (Nashville, TN: W Publishing Group, 1996), 197.

10. Bill Moyers, "Blind Faith," *In These Times*, February 9, 2005, http://www.inthesetimes.com/article/1915/blind_faith/.

11. See Psalm 49:3, Psalm 37:30, Psalm 111:10; Proverbs 1:7, Proverbs 2:6, Proverbs 2:10, Proverbs 3:13, Proverbs 4:5, Proverbs 4:7, Proverbs 7:4, Proverbs 8:1, Proverbs 8:12, Proverbs 10:13, Proverbs 11:2, Proverbs 13:10, Proverbs 14:6, Proverbs 14:8, Proverbs 15:33, Proverbs 19:8, Proverbs 23:23, Proverbs 31:26; Ecclesiastes 1:16.

Chapter 3. Our Green Creator-God

1. This is neither a complete assent to narrative theology or a denial of the propositional truth of God's word. It is a mere affirmation of the narrative structure of much of the Old Testament.

2. Much of the Bible is an ancient storybook, although it is not only that. It is overflowing with propositional truth and principles for right living.

3. N. T. Wright, *Surprised by Hope: Rethinking Heaven, the Resurrection, and the Mission of the Church* (New York: HarperOne, 2008) 94.

4. I don't usually pray to "Jehovah-fill-in-the-blank," and I'm not particularly elated when a church choir sings a thirteen-minute arrangement of the latest praise song while the ushers bring in elaborately decorated banners with God's names sewn on them.

5. Walter Bruggeman, *Genesis* (Louisville, KY: John Knox Press, 1982), 24.

6. One of the elements about biblical Hebrew that is both fascinating and frustrating is the absence of punctuation. No periods, no question marks, no commas. If you were to read the Old Testament Scriptures in their original form, you would

simply find page upon page of odd-looking letters. In English, we jot down an exclamation point. In Hebrew, one would simply repeat a word to add intensity and significance.

7. John Calvin, *Genesis Commentary*, ed. Alister McGrath and J. I. Packer (Wheaton, IL: Crossway Books, 2001), 28.

8. See Steve Monsma, *Healing for a Broken World: Christian Perspectives on Public Policy* (Wheaton, IL: Crossway Books, 2008), 33.

9. R. Kent Hughes, *Genesis: Beginning and Blessing* (Wheaton, IL: Crossway Books, 2004), 15.

Chapter 4. Dominion as Benevolent Monarchy

1. Fowler, *Greening*, 156.

2. John H. Walton, *The NIV Application Commentary: Genesis* (Grand Rapids, MI: Zondervan, 2001), 132.

3. The term *benevolent king* is borrowed from Bruce Waltke, *Genesis: A Commentary* (Grand Rapids, MI: Zondervan, 2001), 67.

4. Abraham Kuyper, *A Centennial Reader*, ed. James D. Bratt (Grand Rapids, MI: Wm. B. Eerdmans Publishing Co., 1998), 461.

5. Nahum Sarna, ed., *The JPS Torah Commentary: Genesis* (Philadelphia: Jewish Publication Society, 1989), 12–13.

6. Loren Wilkinson, *Earthkeeping in the Nineties* (Eugene, OR: Wipf & Stock Publishers, 2003), 209.

7. Tremper Longman III and David Garland, eds., *The Expositor's Bible Commentary: Genesis—Leviticus* (Grand Rapids: Zondervan, 2008), 79–80.

8. See Monsma, *Healing*, 39.

9. See Francis A. Schaeffer and Udo Middelmann, *Pollution and the Death of Man* (Wheaton, IL: Crossway Books, 1970), 71.

Chapter 5. Unexpected God-Moments

1. See Steven Bouma-Prediger, *For the Beauty of the Earth: A Christian Vision for Creation Care* (Grand Rapids, MI: Baker Academic, 2001), 149.

2. Tri Robinson with Jason Chatraw, *Saving God's Green Earth* (Boise, ID: Ampelön Publishing, 2006), 109.

3. For more on this, see Christopher Wright, *The Mission of God: Unlocking the Bible's Grand Narrative* (Downers Grove, IL: InterVarsity Press, 2006), 326.

4. Random funny fact: On occasion, the Georgia National Wildlife Federation and Garden Club will team up to work on an environmental issue. They call themselves "Guns and Roses Coalition."

5. See Calvin DeWitt, *Earth-Wise: A Biblical Response to Environmental Issues* (Grand Rapids, MI: CRC Publications, 1994), 43.

6. Schaeffer and Middelmann, *Pollution*, 75.

7. Robinson with Chatraw, *Saving*, 21.

8. Frank E. Gaebelein, ed., *The Expositor's Bible Commentary: Psalms, Proverbs, Ecclesiastes, Song of Songs* (Grand Rapids: Zondervan, 1991). Cf. Deuteronomy 25:4.

9. As quoted in Willis J. Jenkins, *Ecologies of Grace: Environmental Ethics and Christian Theology* (Oxford: Oxford University Press, 2008), 168.

10. As quoted in Tony Campolo, *How to Rescue the Earth Without Worshiping Nature: A Christian's Call to Save Creation* (Nashville, TN: Thomas Nelson Publishers, 1992), 58.

11. David Gushee, "The Sanctity of All Life," *Creation Care Magazine*, Fall 2008, 42.

Chapter 6. The Sanctuary in Which We Live

1. Barbara Brown Taylor, *An Altar in the World: A Geography of Faith* (New York: HarperOne, 2009), 5–6.

2. As told in Bill Hybels's sermon, "Big Questions Our World Must Answer, Part 2: Can Our Planet Survive," *Creation Care for Pastors*, http://www.creationcareforpastors.com/sermons.

3. John R. W. Stott, *The Message of Romans* (Downers Grove, IL: InterVarsity Press, 2001), 74.

4. For more on nature-deficit disorder, see Richard Louv, *Last Child in the Woods: Saving Children from Nature-Deficit Disorder* (Chapel Hill, NC: Algonquin Books, 2008).

5. Albert Mohler, "Avoiding 'Nature-Deficit Disorder'—It's About Theology, Not Therapy," June 5, 2007, http://www .albertmohler.com/blog_read.php?id=957.

6. Job 37–41; 42:5; See Stott, *Message of Romans*, 73.

Chapter 7. Skeptics, Cynics, and New York Times Bestsellers

1. Al Gore Support Center, 2008, http://algoresupportcenter.com/ accomplishments3.html#anchor_50.

2. Ben Lowe, *Green Revolution: Coming Together to Care for Creation* (Downers Grove, IL: InterVarsity Press, 2009), 124.

3. Inspired by my essay, "Red, Blue and Green," in Lowe, *Green Revolution*.

4. Todd Strandberg, "Bible Prophecy and Environmentalism," *Rapture Ready*, n.d., http://www.raptureready.com/rr-environ mental.html.

5. Wright, *Surprised*, 119.

6. Schaeffer and Middelmann, *Pollution*, 81.

7. "Falwell Says Global Warming Tool of Satan," http://talk
.livedaily.com/showthread.php?t=570478.

8. Alister McGrath, *The Open Secret: A New Vision for Natural Theology* (Hoboken, NJ: Wiley-Blackwell, 2008), 118.

9. Wright, *Mission*, 113.

10. Philip Yancey, "A Whole Good World Outside: Opening Our Blinds to the Prevailing Wonder of Creation," *Christianity Today*, July 6, 2009, http://www.christianitytoday.com/ct/2009/july/15.64.html?start=1.

11. Alister McGrath, *The Reenchantment of Nature: The Denial of Religions and the Ecological Crisis* (New York: Doubleday & Co., 2003), 49.

12. Bouma-Prediger, *For the Beauty*, 125.

13. For more on this, see Alister E. McGrath, *Open Secret: A New Vision for Natural Theology* (Hoboken, NJ: Wiley-Blackwell, 2008), 115–33.

14. As quoted by McGrath, *Reenchantment of Nature*, 51.

15. Wright, *Mission*, 113.

Chapter 8. Facing the Facts

1. Jonathan M. Katz, "Poor Haitians Resort to Eating Dirt," *National Geographic*, January 30, 2008, http://www.news.nationalgeographic.com/news/2008/01/080130-AP-haiti-eatin.html.

2. Candice Eaches, "A Green Revolution," *Off the Vine*, no. 5 (Spring 2009): A1.

3. Charles Mann, "Our Good Earth," *National Geographic*, September 2008, 88.

4. Wes Jackson and Wendell Berry, "A 50-Year Farm Bill," *New York Times*, January 4, 2009, http://www.nytimes.com/2009/01/05/opinion/05berry.html?_r=1&ref=opinion.

5. Thomas L. Friedman, *Hot, Flat, and Crowded* (New York: Farrar, Straus and Giroux, 2008), 46.

6. http://panda.org/about_our_earth/about_forests/problems/.

7. As cited in DeWitt, *Earth-Wise*, 35.

8. http://soils.usda.gov/use/worldsoils/papers/land-degradation-overview.html.

9. "Half Full," GOOD Magazine (Summer 2009), 33, http://www.good.is/post/half-full/.

10. http://www.worldwatercouncil.org/index.php?id=25,http://www.worldwaterday.org/wwday/2001/report/ch0.html.

11. As cited in Robinson with Chatraw, *Saving*, 60.

12. http://www.pcrf.org/reeffacts.html.

13. http://creationcare.org/resources/sunday/facts.php.

14. Ibid.

15. http://www.who.int/mediacentre/factsheets/fs313/en/index.html.

16. http://www.unep.org/urban_environment/issues/urban_air.asp.

17. http://www.who.int/mediacentre/news/notes/2007/np20/en/index.html.

18. http://www.ncm.org/awareness/environment/pollution.

19. http://www.esrl.noaa.gov/gmd/aggi/.

20. As cited in DeWitt, *Earth-Wise*, 36.

21. http://panda.org/about_our_earth/biodiversity/biodiversity/.

22. http://panda.org/about_our_earth/all_publications/living_planet_report/living_planet_index/.

23. http://panda.org/about_our_earth/about_freshwater/freshwater_problems/.

24. oceana.org/fileadmin/oceana/.../Reports/SOWF_document_070907.pdf

25. http://creationcare.org/resources/sunday/facts.php

26. Ray Robinson, *Famous Last Words: Fond Farewells, Deathbed Diatribes, and Exclamations upon Expiration* (New York: Workman Publications, 2003).

Chapter 9. The Enemy in Us All

1. http://www.answers.com/topic/walt-kelly.

2. Friedman, *Hot*, 21.

3. Ibid., 3.

4. Maryanne Vollers, "Razing Appalachia," *Mother Jones*, July/August 1999, http://www.motherjones.com/politics/1999/07/razing-appalachia; for a distinctly Christian perspective on this, see Christians for the Mountains, www.christiansforthemountains.org.

5. http://www.marshall.edu/library/speccoll/virtual_museum/buffalo_creek/html/default.asp.

6. As quoted in the film *Renewal*, http://www.renewalproject.net/.

7. Kathy Marks and Daniel Howden, "The World's Rubbish Dump: A Tip That Stretches from Hawaii to Japan," *Independent*, February 5, 2008, http://www.independent.co.uk/environment/the-worlds-rubbish-dump-a-garbage-tip-that-stretches-from-hawaii-to-japan-778016.html.

8. Read more in the following article: Justin Berton, "Continent-Size Toxic Stew of Plastic Trash Fouling Swath of Pacific Ocean," *San Francisco Chronicle*, October 19, 2007, http://www.sfgate.com/cgi-bin/article.cgi?f=/c/a/2007/10/19/SS6JS8RH0.DTL&hw=pacific+patch&sn=001&sc=1000#ixzz0S3O6zxpGh ttp://www.sfgate.com/cgi-bin/article.cgi?f=/c/a/2007/10/19/SS6JS8RH0.DTL&hw=pacific+patch&sn=001&sc=1000.

9. Robert Malone, "Dirtiest Cities Just Get Dirtier," *Forbes.com*, March 21, 2007, http://www.forbes.com/2007/03/21/worlds dirtiest-cities-biz-logistics-cx_rm_0321dirtiest.html.

10. Eaches, "Green Revolution," A1.

11. Ibid.

12. http://www.dosomething.org/tipsandtools/11-facts-about pollution.

13. http://www.wsmh.com/community/green_team/recycle_rea sons.shtml.

14. Eaches, "Green Revolution," A1.

15. Central Intelligence Agency, *The World Factbook*, 2007, https://www.cia.gov/library/publications/the-world-factbook/rankorder/217+rank.html.

16. Friedman, *Hot*, 80.

17. International Institute for Environment and Development as quoted in "Outline for Educating for Sustainable Living," University of South Carolina (www.sc.edu/sustainableu/SustainableLiving2.pdf).

18. "Amazon Deforestation Trend on the Increase," *Science Daily*, January 6, 2009, http://www.sciencedaily.com/releases/2009/01/090104093542.htm.

19. http://rainforests.mongabay.com/20neotropical.htm.

20. Ibid.

21. Jared Diamond, *Collapse: How Societies Choose to Succeed or Fail* (New York: Penguin, 2005), 4.

22. Wermer Fomos, "A Global Concern: A Population Crisis Still Looms," *New York Times*, January 14, 2004, http://www.nytimes.com/2004/01/14/opinion/14iht-edfornos_ed3_.html.

23. http://www.worldwatercouncil.org/index.php?id=25.

24. Friedman, *Hot*, 56.

25. Ibid.

26. John De Graaf, Thomas H. Naylor, and David Wann, *Affluenza: The All-Consuming Epidemic* (San Francisco: Berrett-Koehler Publishers, 2005), 3.

27. Friedman, *Hot*, 66.

28. Ibid., 6.

Chapter 10. Do These Jeans Make My Landfill Look Fat?

1. http://www.travelersdigest.com/top_dangerous_locations.htm.

2. Robert McFadden and Angela Macropoulos, "Wal-Mart Employee Trampled to Death," *New York Times*, November 28, 2008.

3. In response, some people have begun celebrating Buy Nothing Day on the infamous Friday: https://www.adbusters.org/campaigns/bnd.

4. De Graaf, Taylor, and Horsey, *Affluenza*, 1.

5. Ibid., 2.

6. Ibid., 13.

7. Juliet B. Schor, *The Overspent American: Why We Want What We Don't Need* (New York: HarperPerennial, 1998), 65.

8. "U.N. Study: Americans Work More," Associated Press, September 1, 2001, http://www.foxnews.com/story/0,2933,33487,00.html.

9. Friedman, *Hot*, 66.

10. Jeanne Marie Laskas, "This Is Paradise," *GQ* (May 2008): 199.

11. Friedman, *Hot*, 71.

12. Mark Bittman, "Rethinking the Meat Guzzler," *New York Times*, January 27, 2008, http://www.nytimes.com/2008/01/27/weekinreview/27bittman.html? r=1.

13. Steven M. Wise, *An American Trilogy: Death, Slavery, and Dominion on the Banks of the Cape Fear River* (Philadelphia: Da Capo Press, 2009), 101.

14. Bryan Walsh, "America's Food Crisis and How to Fix It," *Time*, August 31, 2009, 31.

15. Bittman, "Rethinking."

16. Sidney Poitier, *Life Beyond Measure: Letters to My Great-Granddaughter* (San Francisco: HarperOne, 2008).

Chapter 11. How Green Is Green Enough?

1. "Environmental Trade-Offs," *Washington Post*, n.d., http://www.washingtonpost.com/wp-dyn/content/graphic/2009/04/16/GR2009041600093.html.

2. "Environmental Trade-Offs," web.extension.uiuc.edu/clark/downloads/14744.pdf.

3. It's important to note that the coal-fired power plant that produces my electricity would release much more mercury to the environment if I hadn't made the switch. By learning to recycle my compact fluorescents at the end of their lives, I keep a lot of mercury pollution out of the environment.

4. Oswald Chambers, *My Utmost for His Highest*, "The Price of the Vision," http://www.myutmost.org/070713.html.

5. Schaeffer and Middelmann, *Pollution*, 93.

6. A great example of this is the "Let's Raise a Million Campaign" near my hometown. They have connected energy production to asthma rates among Atlanta's African-American community (www.letsraiseamillion.org).

7. Schaeffer and Middelmann, *Pollution*, 74.

Chapter 12. Something's Rumbling

1. William McKenzie, "Younger Evangelicals Are Taking Movement in a New Direction: Evangelicalism Is Undergoing Both a Generational and Thematic Shift, Says William McKenzie," *Dallas Morning News*, March 18, 2008, http://www.aegis.com/news/dmn/2008/DM080303.html.

Appendix 2. The Big, Bad Climate Question

1. See Spencer Weart, *The Discovery of Global Warming*, rev. and exp. ed. (Cambridge, MA: Harvard University Press, 2008).

2. http://nationalacademies.org/onpi/06072005.pdf; http://www.royalsociety.org/displaypagedoc.asp?id=13619.

3. As referenced in Auden Schendler, "Climate Revelations," *Orion Magazine*, Jan–Feb 2009, http://www.orionmagazine.org/index.php/articles/article/4233/>.

ABOUT THE AUTHOR

JONATHAN MERRITT is a faith and culture writer who has published more than one hundred articles in respected national publications such as *USA Today*, the *Atlanta Journal-Constitution*, *Newsweek*'s "On Faith" blog and *Relevant*, *HomeLife*, *Outreach*, and *Charisma* magazines. As a respected Christian voice, he has been interviewed by ABC *World News*, NPR, PBS *Religion and Ethics Newsweekly*, the *Guardian*, the *New York Times*, and the *Washington Post*.

Jonathan first began speaking out on the divine plan for our planet after a classroom epiphany prompted him to organize a national coalition of Christian leaders who care about creation, founding the Southern Baptist Environment and Climate Initiative. Jonathan holds a bachelor of science degree from Liberty University, a master of divinity degree from Southeastern Baptist Theological Seminary, and a master of theology degree from Emory University's Candler School of Theology. Jonathan is a sought-after speaker for colleges, seminaries, churches, and conferences on cultural and religious issues.

He resides outside of Atlanta, Georgia, and would love to connect with you at jonathanmerritt.com.